D0849689

Michael Berry

Susan Giffin

AuthorHouse™
1663 Liberty Drive, Suite 200
Bloomington, IN 47403
www.authorhouse.com
Phone: 1-800-839-8640

First published by AuthorHouse 5/7/2007

ISBN: 978-1-4343-1513-7 (sc)
     978-1-4343-1512-0 (hc)

Printed in the United States of America
Bloomington, Indiana

This book is printed on acid-free paper.

Cover photograph of Michael Berry by Joe Vaas

Preface

Biographies come in many sizes and styles. Some are written as lofty histories, while others dwell candidly on controversy. In *Michael Berry*, a truly remarkable American of Arab descent, we tap his penchant for storytelling, reliving episodes of his life with ease and simplicity. No need for complex language; he lived his life straightforward, leaving no puzzles as to how he achieved his success. There are no intricate mysteries to unravel, no depths to plumb. This makes the biographer's work much easier.

So, on one hand, we have Michael Berry's memories and on the other, the accolades of his followers. And they are legion. But how does the biographer cover the spectrum of this hero's active and accomplished life? We have chosen to divide the book into sections, each representing an important part of his life. Photographs, old and new, set the tone of each new section and offer a glimpse into the personal and professional life of this truly exceptional human being.

One additional note: The narrative text that introduces stories and bridges the various chapters and sections is the author's creation, unless otherwise indicated.

A biography also serves as a legacy; in this case a living legacy. We recognize his great attributes – strong faith, deep love of family and friends, dogged perseverance in work, and unwavering commitment to community service, whether narrow brushstrokes of local aid or broad sweeps of humanitarianism that bridge vast oceans and faraway continents. We would serve his legacy well to carry his torch to bring greater light to people the world over.

Acknowledgements

The author wishes to express sincere appreciation to many people who made this book possible. To Warren David of David Communications for introducing her to Michael Berry; and to Michael Daher, Ph.D., English Literature instructor at Henry Ford Community College, who started this work several years ago.

The following people opened their hearts and memory banks and thereby contributed significantly to *Michael Berry*:

Ismael Ahmed, Executive Director, ACCESS
Andrea Awada, Principal, Geer Park Elementary School
Alex Balooly, restaurateur
Court of Appeals Judge George Bashara (deceased)
Linda Bazzi
Alec Berry, B. A.
Brendan Berry
Cindy Hanes Berry
David Berry
Gail Berry, M.A.
Laura Berry, J.D., Esq.
Lila Berry
Timothy Berry
Frank Bewick, Publisher, Dearborn Times Herald
Vince Bruno, Special Assistant to the President, HFCC
Sandra Amen Bryan
State Senator Irma Clark-Coleman
UAW Administrator Clarence Contratto (retired)
Edward Deeb, President, Michigan Food & Beverage Association
The Honorable John Dingell, United States Congressman
Circuit Court Judge Charles Farmer (retired)
John L. Francis, J.D., Esq.
Russ Gibb, television journalist and educator

Dearborn Mayor Michael Guido (deceased)
Commissioner Grace Hampton (retired)
    Wayne County Road Commission
Nadia Hider, pharmacist
Avery Jackson, Ph.D.
Frank Kelley, Michigan Attorney General Emeritus
Patricia Kelley, high school teacher
Cindi Berry LaCroix, DVM
Diana Larson
The Honorable Mona Majzoub, U. S. Federal Magistrate
Hussein Makled
Assistant Administrator Bette Misuraca (retired)
    Wayne County
Brian Mosallam
Gerald Nassar
Barry Seifman, J.D., Esq.
Charles Shamey
Arman Simone, J. D., Esq.
Kamal "Kal" Turfah
Professor Al Turfe
Professor Tallal Turfe
Carol Berry Ward
Diane Wazney
Deputy Director Mike Zolik (retired)
    Wayne County Road Commission

Special appreciation also to Steve Ghannam of Mosaic Design Group in Dearborn, Michigan, for his design and layout of this book; to Vid Beldavs at AuthorHouse in Bloomington, Indiana, for his wise counsel throughout the publishing process; and to the AuthorHouse design staff for their finishing touches on the book prior to publication.

Table of Contents

Introduction

Some people acquire leadership skills throughout their lifetime; others are born leaders. Michael Berry, JD, is one such person. From his early life, we learn of his self-assurance, strength, and seriousness of purpose, all requisites of great leadership.

His career in law exemplified the finest in that profession, all too often riddled with controversy and criticism. He practiced law by the books and earned the respect of his associates and clients.

Michael entered the realm of politics – local, district, state, and national – and again his service in that arena elevated him to a stature all too seldom seen. He proudly pioneered where no other Arab American had served and opened doors for those who now enjoy elective office. There again, he earned admiration and respect that has stood the test of time.

His service on the Wayne County Road Commission, especially as its chairman from 1967 to 1983 for the most part eclipsed the criticism that often attends positions of that nature. He proved that he was a man of principle, and he ran the Road Commission from that strong foundation. The only criticism was borne out of jealousy and a feeble attempt to taint Michael's unrivaled success, to no avail.

We share Michael's passions – his family, his horses and his classic cars – and admire his resilience and strength of character. We alternately laugh and cry, tapping the pride he felt at winning a horse race, feeling the joy he experienced as the father of four remarkable daughters, suffering the horrific murder of his beloved first wife, raising a new family, and finding love later in life.

Finally, in league with countless organizations, we applaud Michael Berry's humanitarianism, community activism, and generous service to mankind. He stands as one of the tallest pillars in the Arab American community, an example of the success that follows perseverance, strict adherence to integrity, trust, love, and honor.

For contemporaries and for generations yet born, Michael Berry stands as a beacon to all who cherish freedom and justice, peace and tranquility, success, and the finer things in life. He has shown how to abide by one's faith, while honoring those that believe differently and to take pride in one's heritage without being prejudiced against those of other ethnic backgrounds. He has taught us well, and we would honor him best by following his example.

More than a biography, *Michael Berry* is a well-earned tribute to an extraordinary American.

The
Early
Years

*My country owes me nothing. It gave me, as it gives every boy
and girl, a chance. It gave me schooling, independence of action,
opportunity for service and honor. In no other land could a boy
from a country village, without inheritance or influential friends,
look forward with unbounded hope.*

Herbert Hoover
United States President
1874-1964

Tibnin, Lebanon, 1969

Chapter 1

Michael Berry has been called a pioneer, trailblazer, godfather, mentor, prince, patriarch, and even a prophet, but his early struggles and setbacks were unlikely indicators of the destiny he eventually fulfilled. He was born into poverty, enhanced soon afterward by the dire effects of the Great Depression, and early in life he faced difficulties that drove many to despair. His positive outlook and determination to rise to great heights came, in part, from his remarkable parents, Mohamed and Mariam.

The Berry ancestral roots run deep in the rich soil around Tibnin, a beautiful village in south Lebanon. Built on a hill 20 miles from the sea, Tibnin enjoys moderate temperatures, perfect for growing everything from pears to pomegranates, omnipresent olives, a plentiful array of vegetables and, eventually, tobacco, when villagers realized the boost it would bring to their economy. Tibnin has also been famous for its magnificent crusader castle, built strategically in the hills in 1105 for the purpose of capturing the city of Tyre and in later years invaded by children at play.

Tibnin is known for tolerance, too. Muslims and Christians live together, and the children of both faiths attend school together, although each has their own mosque or church for worship. The tolerance and respect for religious practices steeped in this small village, far from Michael's upbringing and fostered by his parents, became part of the principles by which Michael has conducted his life.

Mohamed took the name Charles when he immigrated to the United States in 1904. He had set sail by steamship from Beirut, traveling to Marseilles, France and then to the United States in a journey that took the better part of a month.

He settled in Highland Park, a cosmopolitan enclave with 49 distinctive ethnic groups, thanks to Henry Ford, who issued open invitations for people to work in his auto manufacturing plants.

There was a sizable Arab community in Highland Park, as well.

The Lebanese immigrants were known as Syrians, according to Chuck Shamey, whose family grew up alongside Michael's. "We didn't use the term Lebanese then. We all were – are – Syrian. Geographically, the West changed that. Most of these families started out in Michigan City, Indiana, but eventually they came to Highland Park to work with Ford. The Arab neighborhood there bustled with falafel street vendors and children at play."

Highland Park enjoyed two remarkable distinctions in those days. "It was the third cleanest city in the United States," says Dr. Avery Jackson. "They used to not only sweep the streets but also the alleys once a month and they washed them down." The city was also noted for having the third highest education standard in the country.

Over the next five years, Charles Berry set about working hard and saving money to start a family. He applied his skills as a tool grinder for Ford Motor Company, first in Highland Park and later in Dearborn, eventually retiring after 40 years of service.

Every once in a while, old man Henry Ford would come down the line and say, "Willie, follow me." Ford would give him something to do…a tool to make…and Charles would make it for him. "My father had extra super vision…real vision," Michael recalls. "He very seldom had to use a micrometer to check his work. He really had the feel for his job. He was self taught on the prints to grind the tolerances that Ford required."

In 1909, Charles returned to Lebanon and married Mariam Salah, returning to the States alone. She followed the next year, 1910, arriving to find her new husband in the hospital due to injuries from a motorbike accident.

Ten years later, on May 8, 1920, Michael became the fourth child born to Mohamed and Mariam Berry in Highland Park, Michigan. Michael joined the first two children in the family, Edna, the eldest, and Henry. One other child, born two years before Michael, passed away before he arrived. Michael and his brother and sister eventually welcomed six other siblings – Amy, Jim, Lindy, Amira, Frank, and Patricia. "Lindy was named after Charles Lindbergh," Patricia explains. "Our parents pretty much named each of us after an American patriot, because that was their way of assimilating into the American culture."

Michael's earliest memories reveal humor and ambition. The snuff story is one such story. "A fellow second grader, named Gus, told me

Mariam and Charles Berry [circa 1918]

during morning recess that he had some snuff," recalls Michael. In those days, men used to put a pinch of snuff on the top of their closed fist and sniff it up their nose, then sneeze. Gus explained, 'If we do that, we will get sick and have to go home, and then we can play marbles.'

"Well, we sniffed the snuff. I got nauseous. When we returned to class, I told the teacher I felt sick. So did Gus. She sent both of us to the school nurse. She popped a thermometer in my mouth, and one in Gus's mouth. The nurse stepped outside momentarily, and while she was gone, Gus thought he would outsmart her, so he put the thermometer on the radiator to give it some real heat. I kept mine in my mouth.

"When the nurse returned, she looked at Gus's thermometer, and then slapped his face and sent him back to class. She then looked at mine and saw that I was running a low-grade temperature and sent me home. Alas! The trick worked, but I had no playmate."

Another early memory speaks more to a different kind of ambition. On the corner of Woodward and Manchester, Judge Cody, a Christian Lebanese, before he became a judge had the newspaper concession. Newspapers sold for three cents. For two years, from age 7 to 9, Michael sold the Detroit Times, Detroit News, and Detroit Free Press. Judge Cody would give him papers, and Michael would hawk them on the streets.

"Imagine a seven-year-old yelling *Extra! Extra!* There was no extra! Except in tips; occasionally someone would give me a nickel, which was enough to buy a hot dog at the stand on Victor at Woodward [that hot dog stand is still there today]. They were great hot dogs. Occasionally, I would accumulate ten cents and get a hamburger."

Nadia Hider, one of Michael's current neighbors, loves hearing Michael tell how his mother would admonish him after he misbehaved: *"Ma btswa kishrit basle* – You aren't going to be worth an onion peel." Years later, of course, as he received one of many of his awards, he is known to have said, "Mother, I wonder what you would think of me now."

Mariam Berry was a great wife, wonderful mother, and homemaker par excellence. Known for her open kitchen, deep affection, and great sense of humor, she was outgoing and fun to be around.

"Her grape leaves and stuffed squash were the greatest," Michael remembers fondly. "I used to help her in the kitchen on weekends. She would bake the bread and meat pies. When my friends came over, they knew that they could sit down and she would serve them. She was that kind of person."

Arman Simone, who eventually studied law with Michael, fell in love with Michael's mother and his sister, Amy. "Everyone should have a mother like Mariam," he says. "She was oozing with love and always doing service for others. She was always saying 'you have to help people', and Michael just jumped on that."

In addition to being warm and outgoing, she was also intelligent. Michael used to think his father had the most to say and command but, in retrospect, he now believes his mother was the influencing factor in the family. "She was also the disciplinarian. My father was the last resort. When he raised his voice, we responded accordingly."

Pictured with Charles Berry: L to R, standing: Henry and Michael, L to R, sitting: Amy, Jim, and Lindy

"When Mike talks about his father back at the turn of the last century and all that he did," says Chuck Shamey, "I get a good feeling for how American his father really was, how closely he related to the American way of life. I believe that filtered down to Mike. He derived a lot of strength and character from his parents. He was an American first."

In 1930, Charles decided to take the entire family to Lebanon so that his children could see first hand the beauty of the land he so loved and introduce them to their rich heritage and extended family.

"Our parents had not prepared us for what we should expect," Michael recalls. "They used to tell us about their homeland, stories about hyenas at night on the outskirts of the village and so on, but they never mentioned anything about not having running water or heat or electricity or gas. I took it for granted that these things existed."

The SS Byron, a 10,000-ton freighter – one-tenth the size of today's luxury cruise ships – carried passengers, like the Berry family, to distant shores. The trip from New York to Beirut took 23 days. "Onboard ship, there was nothing at all to do, except throw up, which I did frequently. The trip was sickening. Our first stop was Lisbon, Portugal. My father and I walked down onto the wharf, where the fishermen were displaying some of their catch for the day – red snapper, I believe they were. Dad bought several of them, and my mother cleaned and prepared them for cooking. She asked the cooks onboard if she could cook the fish for us. They allowed her to do that, and we had a good dinner, better than what they provided us on the ship."

After arriving in Beirut, Michael, 10, and his sister, Amelia, about 7, went ahead of the rest of the family to Tibnin, the village where their parents were born. "It was Amy's and my fault that we went early. We were so eager to see the village, so my Dad said, 'If you want to go, go ahead.' And so we went. I've regretted it ever since."

The two youngsters went by car to a certain point where the road ended at a small village south of Beirut. There, they met up with a train of pack animals. "They took some of our luggage and put it on one of the donkeys and then they put Amy and me on a mule. We rode that way for several hours into the night until we reached Tibnin. Probably around 30 or 40 people traveled with us. That was the mode of transportation back in 1929, early 1930.

"On the mule train ride, we saw eyes in the darkness. We were told they were hyenas, which would dog the mule train and follow it. The people who ran the pack train had guns, so we were not really concerned about the animals. We could see their eyes back in the distance, but did not hear any of the hyena's distinctive howling. I never saw one in broad daylight."

When Michael and Amy arrived in Tibnin, their father's brother, Abu Rashad, whom they did not know, met them. "He took us to a place in the village proper where he owned about five or six huts or one-story dwellings. There was also a two-story dwelling, which we might call a condo today. Amy and I climbed the stairs to the room where we found a bed and an incandescent fixture. It was not electrical, but perhaps the kerosene kind that one had to light. It was covered with a shade and was a nice-looking lamp.

"There was no running water. The bathroom facilities were outside, like they were on the farms. Well, I wasn't used to that, and neither was my sister. We cried all night, just the two of us. We were in a strange country, in a strange village, with strangers all around. We had absolutely no knowledge of the people. We did not recognize a single soul."

For the next two days, the two children lived in a frightening atmosphere, although Abu Rashad and his family tried to please them by making food and being otherwise hospitable. "We didn't feel like eating. We were just totally, honestly, in a state of shock."

Finally, the rest of the family arrived. Michael's father owned part of the property there, and on it was a two-unit dwelling. The family occupied one unit, and later Michael used the smaller adjoining unit for breeding a variety of pigeons.

"From that point on, I became accustomed to the lack of facilities, lack of playground, lack of reading materials, and lack of paper. Everything that I had here, the things you would expect to find even in the poorest areas, they didn't have overseas."

Michael was not prepared for the reception he and his family received. "Frankly, I believe they worshipped Americans. They thought the Americans were great; in fact, everyone wanted to go to America. It was the land not only of freedom but also the place where they could excel, where they could have better living conditions, and so forth. They had heard so many stories; anyone who came to the village from America was treated like a deity.

"After a few months, I got into the scheme of things and started playing with my classmates and others. We would go up to the ancient crusader fortress, which still exists. We used to play make-believe war games."

In some ways it was an exciting time for young Michael, but not when it came time for him to help out, doing things he had to do. "Like when it was my turn to fetch water; things like that got to be chores, especially when I wanted to play, and I was forced – and I mean literally forced – to do them.

"To get water, I had to travel two or three miles by donkey or mule, whichever was available. The animal was outfitted with two bamboo baskets, one on each side, with huge earthen jars, which held about five gallons each. I would go to the well that the government had constructed and fill the earthen jars from the well."

Michael also watched with fascination the harvesting of wheat and transporting of it to the local grist mill. "A huge single-cylinder engine had a wheel that stood about six feet tall. The engine had a conveyor belt running about 30 feet in length, and it was attached to the grist mill. The harvesters would dump the wheat into the mill, which would then grind it into different textures, coarser for bulgar and finer for flour. Each grind had a different setting. That was very interesting."

Despite having to do chores, Michael considered himself fortunate, because until a year or two before he and his family arrived, there had been no schools in Tibnin. "Lebanon – or Syria, as it was known then – was a French mandate. The school was a one-classroom building attached to the mosque. The only teacher – Mu'aalam Ali – was a pretty competent man, because he was able to handle 20 to 30 students, ranging from 7 years to 20 years of age."

Michael learned Arabic, and in the short period of time he was there, he was able to read and write Arabic. "Prior to that, I had some knowledge of the language, as it was spoken in our household. I had had some schooling in Arabic in Highland Park, too, and that was improved upon in Dearborn, after we returned to the States. After school, a class was held in the basement of one of the families in South Dearborn, and there we were instructed in the reading of the Holy Quran, how to write the alphabet, how to spell, and things like that. That was the extent of my knowledge. I have a basic understanding of Arabic now, and can make out printed material in the language."

Other than difficulty with the language itself, schooling in Tibnin was nothing that one would classify as intermediate studies like Michael and his siblings had in the United States. "They gave us a little bit of art and a little bit of math, as well as spelling, reading, and writing. There was no geography, no history, and no science.

"Math was rather easy for me, because the other students were far behind what I had learned in America, and because the teacher had to instruct the younger students as well as the older ones, who had never had any schooling whatsoever. By the time I arrived in Tibnin, I had already had some of the math courses, and I would translate them; therefore I had a decided advantage due to my studies in public schools in Highland Park."

Michael missed more than America's public schools. "Frankly, I missed everything. I'm talking not only the dress, the people, the outdoor bathroom facilities, the lack of hot water, the need to fetch water, but also the fact that we children had to sleep on mattresses on one level of the house with our parents on another level. Also, the fact that there was no electricity; you didn't just push a button and get light. It was primitive, a primitive existence. Mother had to make dough and bake bread and make our food from scratch. It was not a healthy surrounding, nor was it an easy place to live. Not for my mother or my father and not for any of the kids."

But his parents wanted to stay; they thought they could make a go of it in Lebanon. "We children used to cry and cry and cry and ask to be taken back home to the States. Eventually my father realized that the business he planned to start there – a taxi service – wouldn't pan out."

As the family decided to return to America, Michael realized he would miss little about his stay in Tibnin. "I would miss the pigeons I had raised and a few friends, but they were friends on short notice. I got to know them only for a period of seven or eight months; so they were not the kind of ties like I established in Highland Park and subsequently in Dearborn. Tibnin was not the kind of place I would have recommended to my children or to anybody else. It was not the best of life."

But the experience had given him a closer look at and understanding of the culture and the religion. "I received a feeling for their way of living, but I never cared to repeat it."

More than his personal exposure to the Lebanese ways there, it was his parents who taught him the values that have stood the test of time. "The most important things to them were honesty and to abide by the laws of the United States. And never to smoke or drink. I didn't start smoking until I was 21, and I broke the habit 20 years later. Also important to my folks, even though I loved to play and fool around, was schooling, a good education. That was vital to them, and it became vital to me."

The freighter trip home proved to be not the least bit more pleasant than the trip to Lebanon, although the sights were more interesting. The ship stopped in Palermo, Sicily, in Greece, and Spain, where other Americans came onboard. There were three classes for passengers – first, second, and third. "We were in third class."

Michael caught sight of a French or German submarine while they were still in the Mediterranean and he later saw Gibraltar and some British bi-planes that were stationed there. "We also saw dolphins that would congregate around the ship. As we sailed on, I would watch the dolphins swimming alongside the ship and jumping out of the water. It was a beautiful sight!"

As the ship approached the Statue of Liberty, a man onboard who knew that the Berry family was American, asked Michael to recite the Pledge of Allegiance, which he knew from grade school days. Soon afterward, the ship docked in New York.

"We couldn't afford to take the train, because there were so many of us, so my father bought a 1926 or 1927 Chevrolet, and we drove all the way from New York to Detroit. I marvel at the courage my father and mother mustered to take this trip; and the courage of my father, who probably at the age of 17 came to this country and worked on the railroad in Colorado, in Gary, Indiana in the steel mills, and then in Michigan City for a short time before he heard about Ford Motor Company. I couldn't have done that. I wouldn't have had the courage to leave my parents and make a trip of that nature.

"Coming back to Michigan at the end of 1930, we would stop by an open field, and my mother would build a fire and cook for us. She had the proper utensils with her. We would eat and then get back in the car and move on. We slept in the car, too, like a band of gypsies."

Even before the family left Tibnin, Michael's father already was thinking ahead to another possibility that would enable the family to return to Lebanon. The village grist mill had captured his interest, seriously. Michael was concerned that the family would move back there.

"Even to this day, I make statements that I thank God my Dad brought us back to America, because had I lived there the rest of my life, I would probably have loaded donkeys with sacks of flour and things of that sort. That would have been my future there, because there were no schools of higher learning in Tibnin, only in Beirut, and my father's limited earnings even as a cab driver would have not accommodated my going to a school of higher learning. So, I am thankful we came back to the United States."

And so was Hussein Makled, a native of Tibnin and eventual immigrant resident of Dearborn, who vividly remembers when Michael and his family visited the village. "It was the custom back then for a man to go to America, work for a while, start his family and then return to Lebanon," he explained. "For most of them, it didn't work. They had to come back to the States. In Mike's case, it's a good thing they came back. We gained a great man by having him around."

"Ever since growing up in America, whenever I meet people who complain about their life here, I say, 'Be thankful you have been allowed to live in this country.' I say this to people of my heritage who have come here, who have not enjoyed natural-born citizenship in this country. A lot of them consider that I have betrayed my heritage, which is totally untrue. I just recognized that Lebanon was a third world country, which was controlled by other nations, and one that certainly did not give the best opportunities, especially to the people of the Islamic faith, who were treated differently than those of the Christian faith."

Long after leaving Tibnin, unexpected ties to Tibnin occasionally have arisen, such as this one. "My mother's best friend came from the Christian part of the village," Michael recalls, "and she later moved to Flint, Michigan. Her son, Leo Farhat, and I ended up going to law school together. One day we were talking, and he mentioned that his mother was from Tibnin. I told this to my mother, and she requested that I find out his mother's name. Sure enough, it was her best friend! Leo eventually became the prosecuting attorney for Genesee County."

Rouge Complex Workers (Courtesy of Noah's Deli in Dearborn, Michigan)

Chapter 2

When the family arrived in Highland Park, conditions had deteriorated due to the Depression, which was in full force, so the family stayed with relatives. "My father knew that his job had moved to the Rouge plant in Dearborn, which had only seven or eight families in the South End at that time. We went house hunting every day. Dad finally rented a brick house for about $12 a month. It was a two-family flat, 1913 and 1917 Canterbury. After a year or two, Dad decided to buy the house, and I believe he did so for around $5,400. That's where I lived even after I was married and became a father."

The family was very poor when they lived on Canterbury. Once Michael's mother found a pair of girl's shoes in a basement, and since Michael had none, he had no choice but to wear those shoes. Other kids made fun of him, but he learned early in life not to let jabs knock him down.

Typifying the Lebanese tradition not only of great hospitality but also of taking in extended family members to raise with one's own children, Mariam opened her home and heart to her cousin, Floyd, as well as Harry at the age of five and his sister, Faye. [Floyd eventually was involved in the death march in Bataan in the Philippines, and Harry served in the U. S. Navy. After the Japanese sank two battleships, Harry was left in the sea for several hours until he was rescued. No one knew what Harry did or what kind of sailor he was, except that he was a decorated veteran. He was very, very emotionally affected by his experiences in the war.]

By 1931, the population of Dearborn was experiencing growing pains, thanks to Henry Ford's efforts to bring workers from other countries to work on the assembly lines. The South End was then home mostly to Romanians, but boasted an amazing number of other nationalities, too – 53 in all.

Alec Berry and his family grew up in the same house on Canterbury, an upper and lower flat arrangement. Michael demonstrated his sense of humor early on. "He had a chemistry set at home and one day, we were playing outside and he came out wearing scary goggles that frightened the heck out of me. He has always had a good sense of humor, but more than that, he was the kind of person, even early in his life, that was there for people. That is one of his hallmarks."

Michael attended Salina School from the fifth through the ninth grades. Underscoring his parents drive to have their children work hard for a good education, Michael remembers that at Salina, the teachers awarded students the letter 'S' in gold, silver or bronze, signifying A, B or C grade achievements, respectively. "One afternoon at an awards event, my parents attended, and I was called not as an 'A' student, but a 'B' student and awarded a silver 'S'. Consequently, my father got mad at me. My parents always challenged us to work harder and excel in school."

At Salina back in those days, only one Yemini was in school when Michael was there, and only about 30 Arab students, in sharp contrast to today's Arab representation at Salina. Yemini, who now significantly populate the South End, first settled in Hamtramck and other areas.

As a representative of that minority, Michael first encountered discrimination in the eighth grade by way of Mr. Freeden, a teacher who seemed to favor the fair-skinned students. "For some reason, he didn't like my appearance. I don't recall if he treated other Arab students like he treated me, but many times he made me feel humiliated. I did not feel that I merited that kind of treatment."

Once when Mr. Freeden was absent, the substitute teacher gave Michael an 'A' on an oral quiz of the previous day's assignment, identification of the glands in the mouth. When the substitute asked, "Who can give me the names?" no hands went up. So Michael raised his hand and dutifully recited the glands – sublingual, submaxillary, and so on. The substitute teacher responded by telling Michael he would give him an 'A' not just for that oral quiz but he would also recommend to Mr. Freeden that he receive an 'A' for the rest of the semester. So that was one of Michael's early lessons.

Humiliation can scar a young person or it can instill the value of tolerance. For Michael, it was the latter. He would one day become a champion for people from all walks of life, all colors and creeds. And he learned at a young age how to stand up for the rights of others.

In 1933, Franklin Delano Roosevelt became president. "My father would listen to his fireside chats on the radio every Friday evening.

Everyone had to be absolutely quiet while the president spoke. We would sit around the radio together and listen."

One day, Charles Berry received notice that he was laid off, despite being one of the better tool and die makers at Ford's Rouge plant. So, Charles turned to his son, Michael, and said, "Write to President Roosevelt and tell him what happened to me."

Michael questioned his father's request. "Dad, he's not going to listen to you. He's got other things to do. He's running a whole country. Why would he pay attention to you?"

When his father persisted, Michael finally asked, "Why not ask Henry write the letter?"

"No," his father replied. "You write the letter."

Michael took his cheap school paper and wrote President Roosevelt about his father's lay-off. "I signed my father's name and mailed it."

That was not the end of the story. A couple of weeks later, there was a knock-knock at the door. When Michael answered the door, he saw two men dressed in suits. "Charles Berry live here?" they inquired firmly.

"Yes."

"We would like to speak to him."

They entered the family room, closest to the front door, and started to ask Charles questions. Michael served as translator whenever his father did not understand what the men were saying.

"My father told the men that he had worked for Ford for many years and got laid off, making it tough for us to make it," Michael explains. "He was doing only odd jobs. The men wrote down everything."

Again, Michael figured that was the end of the story. But about 10 days later, Charles Berry received a card in the mail – REPORT TO WORK – FORD MOTOR COMPANY. Same department. Same job.

"That's how responsive President Roosevelt was," Michael recalls. "I hold him in highest esteem. In my opinion, he was the greatest president that ever lived."

[About seven years ago, Dr. Michael Daher, an English literature instructor at Henry Ford Community College, learned that Michael's letter to President Roosevelt has been preserved all these years in the archives of the United States Department of Labor in Washington, D.C., as noted in the Roosevelt Administration archives. That discovery was much to Michael Berry's surprise.]

By the time Michael arrived at Fordson High School in 1936, he had fallen in love – with science. His interest in science grew throughout high school, as did his talent in and respect for the subject, to the point that his parents encouraged him to pursue a career in medicine.

Michael became a lab assistant in his first semester of chemistry with Dr. Max Musser, whom he considered a great and inspiring teacher. "One day, we had a lab experiment in which we filled a test tube with water, and then we dropped a piece of sodium into the water. Well, it blew up in my eyes. I remember Max being quite concerned. He took me to the nurse who washed out my eyes. Fortunately, everything turned out well."

Michael's serious pursuit of science did not interfere with pranks, such as masterminding clever ways of skipping school. "In my days at Fordson, I got involved with a group of boys that was very talented in the ways of skipping school. We did a lot of that."

One day, they went to Ann Arbor. The next day they got caught. Their first class in the morning was Latin with Miss MacMillan. Several of the boys were in her class and as each one entered the room, she asked, "Where were you yesterday?"

Curtis Moore, a redhead, said he was ill. The next one was Fred Nassar. "Where were you yesterday?" the teacher queried. He said he was ill.

Everyone ahead of Michael gave the same response. She then asked Michael where he was the day before. "I was sick," he told her. With that, she was onto them.

The class clown was a blond kid, Eugene Gach, who also explained to Miss MacMillan that he was sick the day before.

"You, too?" the teacher asked.

"Yes," he replied. "It was an epidemic."

The teacher sent them all to the principal's office because she didn't like his answer.

"Eugene couldn't let go," said Michael. "He had to make a funny out of it."

Despite occasional diversions from his schoolwork, Michael became a good student in most subjects. He had high regard for Mr. Brown, his civics instructor. The first day in class, Mr. Brown assigned a chapter in the book for homework.

The next day he asked the class "What is the name given to Eight Mile Road?"

Nobody knew the answer. Michael raised his hand. "Yes?" asked the teacher.

"Baseline Road," Michael responded.

"You got it," Mr. Brown said. "On the basis of what I've seen in this class, you're the only one who's done the work. I'm going to make sure you get an 'A' for the rest of the semester."

Believe it or not, Mr. Brown gave Michael an 'A' for the rest of the semester. "That really hurt me more than it helped me," Michael admitted, "because I figured if I already got an 'A', I didn't have to do anything. But I did some of the work anyway."

In December 1936, life for the Berry family ran into some rough sledding. Charles worked only off and on, compounding the difficulties of raising a large family. Perhaps it was during times like those that Charles Berry decided to pursue his dream of returning to Tibnin and running his own grist mill. He asked Michael to write to several manufacturers of grist mills, including Fairbanks Morse, which also made the single-cylinder engines.

"My father, who was an excellent mechanic, in 1937-38 found one of those engines on a farm and had it hauled to our backyard on Canterbury. He proceeded to dismantle it, repair it, and start it up, much to the dismay of the neighbors. But he got it working, and then he bought the grist mill from Fairbanks Morse and shipped both pieces of equipment overseas just before World War II broke out. Almost 30 years later when I returned to Lebanon, I found the remnants of both the engine and the mill; parts had been stolen and the mill dismantled, and a new mill had replaced it."

Nothing ever came of Charles' dream to move his family back to Lebanon. Michael decided it was time, at age 16, for him to help his family; unfortunately the minimum age for hiring at the Ford plant was 18. He was determined to remedy that problem. Here, he tells that story.

"I took the birth certificate of my deceased brother, who would have been two years older than I, and I changed his first name to mine, magically making me old enough to work. I walked from our house on Canterbury in the South End to Miller Road, and then took Miller Road north to the Ford employment office.

"It was very cold, in fact, bitter, bitter cold. I stood there with blacks, whites and a wide variety of people that populated the south end at that time. The line was a couple of blocks long.

"Out came a big black fellow, who had played football for the University of Michigan. He was obviously a star. Ford had given him a job in the employment office and he went down the line, saying 'You… You…You…' He selected me. Here I weighed all of about 115 pounds. I filled out the application and showed the birth certificate that I proved was of age. I got the job, working on the motor line in the Ford motor building.

"The first two weeks I endured the odor of burnt oil in the morning…and the sweat and odor of co-workers. I became nauseous. The foreman sent me to First Aid, and the nurse would give me a little paper cup with peppermint water to settle my stomach. I would then return to the assembly line.

"It got to the point after two or three days the tips of my fingers were all cut up from the burrs on the nuts that I had to screw onto the cylinder heads. The foreman would come and yell, 'Get going, get going. You're getting behind.'

"At the end of two weeks, I quit. Here, people were lining up to get jobs and I had a job and quit. My mother said, 'That's the best thing that could happen to you. Go back to school.'"

Although not sports-minded in the way most people think of school sports, Michael enjoyed boxing in junior high and high school. "I started out at 115 pounds and went up to 135," says Michael. "I thought I was so good and so fast, that I was willing to take on a guy that weighed 165. He really damaged my image."

Michael never went on to fight professionally, but he retained keen interest in the sport. "He's extremely knowledgeable," says Al Turfe, who has known Michael all his life. "He can go back decades and tell you about a certain boxer, his weight, his reach with a punch, the fights he's won, and all other kinds of information. He has a very excellent memory."

Another career opportunity knocked first, however, in a most surprising way. Michael enjoyed dancing. Peter Krivosheyff, a classmate of Michael's, was a great dancer. They hit all the school dances and became fairly adept at the new dance craze – the Jitterbug.

"Benny Goodman came to town, so we skipped school," Michael tells. "Pete's sister was my dance partner, and he and his girlfriend were partners. When Benny Goodman came on and played, we jumped up onto the stage and danced with our respective partners.

"Afterwards, we received an offer of $70 a week to dance! Now, this was at a time when people were making $6 a day...75 cents an hour, I know for sure." With an offer of $70 a week, Michael went home elated and told his father the good news.

"What kind of offer?" his father asked.

"$70 a week."

His father's eyes lit up. "What are you going to do for $70 a week?" His father, of course, knew that $70 was a lot of money.

"Pete and I and our partners are going to dance," Michael explained casually.

Michael was in the living room. His father was standing in the entry between the kitchen and dining room. He picked up his shoe and threw it at Michael. "I raised you to become a dancer?" he yelled.

That was the end of Michael's prospects of becoming a professional dancer. It was time to turn his sights to more serious pursuits, like medicine.

Michael graduated from Fordson High School in June 1938. High school in those days was three years. Michael finished in two-and-a-half years by attending summer sessions. He had been set back by spending a year in Lebanon, because the schools here did not give him credit for his schoolwork there, but he easily made up for that lost time.

Chapter 3

As fortune had it, Fordson started a junior college and the tuition was very inexpensive. Michael enrolled for the first semester in September 1938.

He had struggled through two years of Latin in high school but fared better in his two years of German in junior college. "I had a wonderful teacher, Miss Horney, who taught at Salina when I was there. She took a liking to me. I had a photographic memory, so I easily memorized the words and translations."

That was when Adolf Hitler was starting to make his moves in Europe. The students would tease her because she was German. On a couple of occasions, she invited Michael to go with her to see some plays in Ann Arbor. "Unfortunately I did not take her up on those invitations. She was wonderful. I hold her in very high esteem.

"What made her a good teacher? She took time to help her students. If they had problems, she would stay after class and explain things to them. She didn't just assign a lesson and that was it."

In the summer of 1940, Michael received his Associate degree as a member of the first graduating class of Fordson Junior College. [Six years later, the school became Dearborn Junior College, and in 1952 Henry Ford Community College. To this day, Michael Berry serves on the foundation board of this fine educational institution.]

Intent on pursuing a career in medicine, Michael applied for a combined curriculum at Wayne State University in 1940, and the university accepted his grades. However, when he appeared before a panel of three doctors, they told him, "We're sorry. We already have accepted 54 students. That is the most we can accept now in our medical school."

"When I realized I could not get into medical school, I decided the hell with it." Instead he attended Wayne State University's Liberal Arts College and finished in 1941. During the time he was going to college, he started a summer program in aeronautics. He received his pilot's license and, believing that war was imminent, applied for the Air Force.

Michael Berry

Graduation, Fordson Junior College, 1940

They sent him to Selfridge Field for a flight examination. He passed a cursory physical exam.

In 1941, he impulsively married Florence, his first love from high school days. The marriage lasted only three months, as World War II broke out and Michael thought it would not be in their best interests to be separated a long time, due to all the uncertainties of war, as he expected to enter military service. Their marriage was annulled. [Due to the shortness of this marriage, for the purposes of this book, we count Michael's next marriage as his first.]

On Sunday, December 7, 1941, Pearl Harbor was attacked. The next

Cousin "Ace" (left) and Michael, 1941

morning, Michael dashed a telegram off to General Hap Arnold, asking to be called immediately into service. That Friday, as he was watching a movie with his girlfriend in the little theater on Dix, his sister Pat rushed in. "There's a telegram at home for you!"

The telegram requested that Michael report the next day. Saturday evening, he was on his way to San Antonio. He was the first to leave home, but perhaps the quickest to return.

"I washed out in the Air Force," he explains. "I had high spinal fluid pressure that gave me severe headaches whenever I flew. The doctors there did a spinal tap, which was very dangerous in those days. In fact, I had two spinal taps, a second one with a doctor on Michigan Avenue in Dearborn after I returned home. I was in the Air Force for only four months." He was honorably discharged.

Not one to give in to defeat, Michael applied to the Navy, but was turned down there, too. "One of the questions on the application for the Naval Air Force was 'Have you ever applied for service?' I answered honestly, and they rejected me forthwith."

Still determined to make some contribution to the war effort, Michael decided that perhaps he could teach flying. He applied and received a memo to go to Curtis Steinbeck Field in East St. Louis, Illinois and take a flight test.

"I had 20 some dollars and I bought a round-trip bus ticket. I couldn't afford to get a room, and since I was scheduled to be there the next day, I had to sleep somewhere, so I went to an all-night theater for a quarter and stayed there.

"The next morning, I washed and shaved in the restroom and then took a bus to the airfield. Believe it or not, I had 20 cents left. I took the flight exam and passed it to fly PT19s, and I bought one after the war. They said they would notify me but they never did.

"I returned home with just enough money to buy a cup of coffee and a nickel to call Henry and ask him to pick me up in downtown Detroit. It was the end at all my attempts at military service."

Vivian Carol Weine, a beautiful and lovely young woman of German heritage, became Michael's wife after he returned from East St. Louis.

To support them, Michael joined Henry in helping their parents with a supermarket they owned on Six Mile Road and San Juan in Detroit.

Due to the war, everything was in short supply. The store had a 75-foot meat counter, but it had no meat. "I watched my parents worry every night about what was going to happen. They had lost all of their money. "

As if the devastating effects of the war were not enough to try Michael's spirit, his first-born son died at Harper Hospital at the age of

Vivian Carol Weine

four months. "That really woke me up," he said. "It was one of the worst days of my life."

The year was 1943. Conditions at the supermarket worsened. People needed ration stamps for food, and certain items ran in short supply. One day, Vivian told Michael, "My uncle is in the meat business. Tomorrow morning you are going with me to the Eastern Market to his slaughter-house."

So, they went on a cold, blustery day. Michael told Vivian to stay in the car. "See if he remembers you," he told her. He then went into the slaughterhouse and asked for her uncle. "Tell him Mike Berry, who married his niece, is here."

The uncle, whom Vivian had not seen in years, came out. "Yes?" he queried.

Michael related the circumstances at his parents' supermarket, noting that at one time the uncle had supplied their market with meat but stopped.

"We'll take care of this," the uncle said. With that, he loaded up Michael's car with two sides of beef. "I'll see to it that the driver makes regular stops at your market," he promised.

As good as that was, it wasn't enough. Michael began to look for additional places to get beef and other meat. He found a cattle farm and became quite adept at selecting cattle. "I'll take this one and that one," he would tell the farmer. He had the cattle shipped to the slaughterhouse and received more than his fair share in return. In addition to selecting prime cattle for slaughter, Michael also worked as a butcher at the family store.

Business really picked up, but then came a shortage of butter. "I saw that customers started to shy away from our store and go to other markets, where they could get butter. One day, I was talking to one of our customers, an elderly gentleman, about our problems."

"I've got a friend who owns a farm in Ohio," the customer offered. "Get your truck ready and we'll go down there."

Off they went in Michael's panel truck to load up with butter. Soon there was plenty of butter to bring customers back. When Thanksgiving approached, and there was no poultry, Michael and the elderly gentleman went to the same farm in Ohio, where Michael bought 3,000 pounds of turkey, dressed. The owner of a nightclub in Detroit heard about the great supply of turkeys and did a lot of business with Michael from then on.

The store was located in an area that attracted such customers as the Winkelman family. Michael and Henry took care of them, and many more families like them.

Finally, the family sold the store in 1946, and Michael and Henry received enough money from their parents – about $1800 – to buy the PT19. The relatively new aircraft, which they located at an airfield in Indiana, had an open cockpit, making the purchase that much more exciting.

Michael Berry, butcher, 1943

"We parked it at Mettetal Airfield in Canton," Michael said. "We owned the plane for a year and a half. It's probably worth 10 times now what we paid for it."

It is interesting how people cross our paths at just the right time to turn us into a new direction. Michael's next experience in a grocery store soon set his sights much higher.

He went to work in the little corner grocery market that his sister, Edna, owned in a predominantly black neighborhood of Detroit. One day, a regular customer came to him and said, "I passed the bar."

Not one to pass up an opportunity to joke around, Michael replied, "I passed a lot of them."

"No, no, Mike," the customer went on, "I passed the bar. I'm now a lawyer."

After the man left, Michael said, "If he can do it, I can do it."

A short time later, Michael and Vivian visited law schools, first Wayne State and then the Detroit College of Law. Michael felt that the atmosphere at the Detroit College of Law was more to his liking, so he applied and was accepted. He entered law school in 1947.

He still needed a job to support his family. Fortunately, Henry, who knew quite a lot about automobiles, opened a used car lot on Vernor in Detroit, and Michael went to work for him.

Their office was in an old converted streetcar and Michael – and his fellow students, Arman Simone and David Anbender – used that office to study law. "Energetic Mike interrupted his studies now and then and went out and sold cars," Arman recalls.

"I was good at it, too," Michael adds. "I delivered 11 cars on a Saturday, under a thousand dollars each."

The brothers enjoyed more than their share of humorous incidents in the course of selling cars. Michael also demonstrated another trait – resoluteness in not compromising his principles. One day, a man came in to look at a convertible. He said he wanted to take it to show his wife, so he did a test drive and came back. Immediately Michael noticed that the tires had been changed.

"You sit right there," he ordered. "I've got your driver's license. You either replace those tires or I'll..."

The man returned to his house, retrieved the four tires, and replaced them on the convertible.

Michael learned from his early practical work experiences and applied those lessons throughout his career. His life has been a true reflection of the wise words of John Fitzgerald Kennedy: "Leadership and learning are indispensable to each other."

Another family business started in early 1950 in Dearborn – Berry's Home Supply – located on Schaefer Road between Ford and Michigan, across from St. Barbara's Catholic Church.

"It was a new business, and our father put up the money to get it off the ground," Patricia recalls. "Lindy and Jim ran the business, and Frank worked there, too. We sold large and small appliances from that location for about five years, and then we moved the store to Joy Road and Inkster. Jim was no longer affiliated with the business. Lindy and Mike became partners. By then, Dad had retired."

The business grew over the next 15 years or more, and stores were opened in Farmington and Ann Arbor, and a furniture store was added to the mix in Redford. "Lindy eventually changed the name to Lucky Lindy's; he made commercials as Lucky Lindy Berry," says Patricia. "Mike was instrumental in so many of the aspects of the business, although he was more or less a silent partner. Because of his law practice and just getting around so much, he brought in so many customers who normally might not have shopped at our stores. Plus, he would always employ nieces and nephews during college breaks."

Lindy, who was the last to hold onto the family business, eventually sold it to ABC Warehouse. He moved to Arizona and opened a store there, and eventually retired.

Law

Practice

The quality of a person's life is in direct proportion to their commitment to excellence, regardless of their chosen field of endeavor.

Vincent T. Lombardi
Great American Football Coach
1913-1970

Chapter 4

With the help of summer sessions, Michael Berry graduated from the Detroit College of Law in 1949, just two-and-a-half years after he enrolled. He earned his Bachelor's degree and eventually his Juris Doctorate (J.D.), and became the first Muslim of Arab descent to practice law in the State of Michigan.

Fresh out of law school, Michael, who admittedly was very naïve about politics, became entangled in the recall movement of Orville Hubbard, mayor of Dearborn. He signed one of the petitions to recall Hubbard, who, despite being an excellent administrator, was known for his hard-line racist stance. Michael was selected – by the Republicans behind the recall – to run the recall office, and they hired a bodyguard to protect him.

"Of course, Mike became a *persona non grata* in Dearborn, especially in the eyes of the mayor," says Vince Bruno, Mike's Italian friend from South End days and now special assistant to the president of Henry Ford Community College. "In those days, they settled matters in different ways than we do today. My wife's uncle – Pasquale Tripepi – became Mike's bodyguard. He went on to wrestle under the names the Masked Marvel and Pepi the Ghost."

"Pasquale was a big guy, who weighed 230 pounds," says Michael. "Whenever he drove me somewhere, he did so almost lying down in the driver's seat. He did that partly to disguise his size. The car we had was a Ford convertible and the sign on the back of the car read RECALL ORVILLE HUBBARD."

One day, Pasquale and Michael were stopped at Michigan and Oakman when a man pulled up alongside them and made a nasty comment about the recall effort.

"You know, if you don't like it, why don't you pull over to the curb?" Pasquale tempted.

They made a left turn and stopped on Michigan near Jonathan. "The other guy pulls right in front of us and got out of his car," Michael says.

Graduation, 1949, Detroit College of Law

"He was a big guy, but so was Pasquale, who was still lying down in his seat. He was wearing heavy parachute boots. The guy came rushing at him, and Pasquale hit him and knocked him down. He tried to get up but by then Pasquale was crushing his head. I said, 'Wait. Let's get the hell out of here; the cops are coming.' And so we did. The guy didn't bother me again."

Eventually, Michael and Orville Hubbard became friends, and at a dinner at the Italian American Club, both men were guest speakers. During Michael's speech, he said, "By the way, Mr. Mayor, you can take my name off the recall petition." Every once in a while after that, Mayor Hubbard challenged Michael to leave his practice and work for him in the city, but Michael chose his own career path wisely.

In an amazing set of circumstances, Michael Berry tried his first lawsuit on December 12, 1949, just days after learning that he passed the bar and a day after being admitted to the Michigan Bar Association. He handled his first case with the same aplomb that marked his entire career.

Michael was working for John D. O'Connell, one of the best trial lawyers in Detroit. "If he had had more business sense, he would have made a hell of a lot more money than he did. He kept everything to himself."

John had mentioned to Michael something about a drunk-driving case that he wanted Michael to handle. The problem was that Michael had not yet taken – or passed – the bar exam.

Michael and Vivian were then a family of three, with the arrival of their first daughter, Laura. They were virtually penniless, so in a desperate move to secure his first case, he went to the dean. "I'm short three hours of being eligible to take the State Bar," Michael told him. "He approved my taking the State Bar anyway.

On December 6th at about 6:00 p.m., Michael received a call that the Bar results were in. He picked up a copy of The Detroit Free Press. "My name wasn't in the Detroit list...then it dawned on me to look under Dearborn and there was my name. I had passed the Bar!"

He immediately relayed the good news to John O'Connell. "Good," he replied, "Go to court and get an adjournment on this drunk-driving case. You can do it now that you're a lawyer."

"But I'm not a lawyer," Michael explained. "I haven't been admitted to the Bar yet."

As it turned out, Michael was admitted to the Bar on the 11th. John sent him to court on the 12th.

Michael did not realize that the traffic court judge had once worked with John O'Connell in the prosecutor's office – two Irishmen under Duncan C. McRae, another Irishman. The two attorneys were constantly at each other's throats.

"John was the better lawyer by far, but the other one was a good political figure, who eventually became traffic judge. John knew that if he went in, he would be in trouble, so he sent me," Michael says.

The case was called. Michael walked up to the front of the courtroom. At this point, he had not yet met his client, who had been charged with drunk driving and property damage.

"Your honor, I'm with Mr. O'Connell's office," he proudly announced. "John D. O'Connell. I respectfully request that the case be adjourned."

"You're from his office?" the judge quizzed.

"Yes, your honor."

"You try it," the judge ordered.

"What?" Michael said, startled.

"You try it," the judge repeated.

Michael knew he had to think fast. The waiting room was full. He had noted that the judge had no jury trials scheduled for that day. "I respectfully request a jury trial, your honor," Michael asserted.

"You've got it," the judge replied.

Michael was floored. Now, the client – a lanky southerner – approached him.

"Go to courtroom such and such," the judge instructed. So Michael and his client proceeded to go downstairs in the Cadillac Tower.

As they did, Michael asked his client to tell him what happened that led to his arrest. The southerner told Michael he was driving a 60,000-pound rig too fast and made a turn onto one of the streets that runs parallel to Vernor.

"I scraped a bunch of cars making the turn and the cops come. When they opened my door, I stumbled, so they took me to the Fort-Green Police Station and booked me on drunk driving."

That's all the information that Michael had to work with. "Do you have any witnesses?" he asked his client.

"No."

All Michael had was the sergeant at the desk at the precinct where the police took his client…and two police officers, who testified that the driver was absolutely drunk and fell out of the cab of his truck. The truck had scraped the cars, not actually collided with them.

On cross-examination, Michael asked for the police to be separated until they were called, so that when they gave testimony, he would cross-examine each one. Fortunately for him, the sergeant was the prosecutor's last witness.

Michael asked the sergeant, "What was the condition of the defend-ant?"

"It's obvious he was drunk. I smelled the liquor."

"Was it strong?" Michael inquired.

"No, it was stale, but I could tell that he'd been drinking."

The other two officers had testified that the liquor odor was strong, so Michael called them back to the courtroom and asked if they had stopped at a bar on the way to the police station and allowed the driver to drink.

The judge started hammering away and told Michael to sit down.

"Yes, your honor." But he had learned some of the tactics John had used in court.

Finally the judge – a stand-in judge from Saginaw – became really peeved at Michael. "Chambers!" the judge ordered. The prosecutor went in, too. The judge instructed, "One more crack out of you and I'll hold you in contempt."

"Your honor," Michael explained, "I'm only trying to cross-examine. I'm not trying to make any wisecracks."

"I'm just warning you," the judge said and dismissed them. When they returned to the courtroom, Michael said in the presence of the jury, "I'd like the record to show that the judge took me into his chambers and intimidated me into trying to limit my cross-examination."

The judge went into such a rage that he had to return to his cham-bers to cool off. When he returned to the courtroom, he said, "One more remark and I'm sending you to jail."

"Yes, your honor." Michael continued his cross-examination. On delivering his side of the case, he said to the jury, "You noticed that I asked the defendant to take out his teeth when he was testifying. You heard him. You saw that he had false teeth and his ability to speak was impaired. [At least, that was the excuse Michael used.] If he was that drunk, he would have demolished all of those cars, because if you take the weight of his vehicle and the speed they claim he was driving, he would have destroyed everything in sight. "

When the jury convened, the southerner turned to Michael and said, "I'll bet you a nickel the jury comes back – guilty." Michael didn't have a nickel, and the jury came back with its verdict: not guilty.

He took the client to John O'Connell's office.

"How did you do?" John asked. "Did you get the adjournment?"

"No, I didn't get the adjournment," Michael teased.

"Well, when are we scheduled for trial?"

"I already had it," Michael informed.

"What happened?"

Michael filled him in on all the details.

"Okay, that's it. You work for the Teamsters," John said. He had an open door with the Teamsters, who sent him all their cases. In fact, at one time, he had been the chief trial lawyer for the prosecutor's office.

Then John said, "Here's $20 for the case you just tried." Michael later checked with the secretary and discovered that John received $300 from the Teamsters for that same case. Michael said to himself, "You can starve on your own; you don't need help."

He told John he would like to rent an office there. John explained that he was not in a position to take on any permanent overhead, so he suggested that Michael talk to Ray LeBar. Michael had never worked for Ray, but he explained his situation to him and found an understanding ear.

"Okay, I'll tell you what," Ray offered, "if you can pay two-thirds – $66 a month – can you do some work for me?"

"I'll be glad to, for nothing," Michael said.

That, in a nutshell, is how Michael Berry started practicing law. He went into business with a loan from his brother Henry, a telephone, a filing cabinet, and Ray Lebar's secretary to do his typing.

He also bought a 1940 Ford, for which he paid about $400. Michael, Vivian, and young Laura were living in a bedroom in the home on Canterbury with his mother.

Michael stayed with Ray Lebar for about a year and a half. Business started to pick up; for one, he was getting all of the kids in the South End that fell into trouble.

One day, a man by the name of Octavius Germany, president of the Homeowners Association of Dearborn's South End, went to see Michael. He represented homeowners in the area where the Edward C. Levy Company planned to build a road, right behind Amazon Street. Ford was selling slag to Edward C. Levy, and he planned to store it right behind their homes.

The homeowners in the area were upset; they complained that the heavy construction trucks were rattling their homes, raising a lot of dust, and disturbing the otherwise peaceful neighborhood. The Homeowners Association wanted something done about it. They had gone to the city, but the city refused to do anything. They went to the prosecutor's office, were refused help there but were referred to a young man by the name of Michael Berry.

The Association had no money but wanted to know if Michael could handle the case. He did not realize immediately the full extent of the case – the Edward C. Levy Company and Ford Motor Company were violating the city zoning ordinance. The City of Dearborn should have taken care of the matter.

Michael ultimately sued the City of Dearborn, Ford Motor Company, and the Ed Levy Company. He then asked for a temporary injunction.

Judge Lila Neuenfeldt, who later went to work for Michael, issued her ruling, "I can't give you a temporary injunction but I will sign a restraining order for two days."

Michael figured that in those two days, he could put some special tactics to work for the homeowners. He called a meeting in the Romanian Hall on Salina, and spoke to the women and their husbands. "I can't tell you what to do, but we must get some publicity and stir up some sympathy for your case. Now, if you women were to block the road…say, stand in the way of the trucks…it might generate some valuable publicity."

Well, sure enough, they formed a human chain across the road. All the trucks tried to get through but couldn't. Of course, photographs were taken of the protest.

Finally, in court, Michael faced opposing counsel, the greatest trial lawyer in Michigan – William Henry Gallagher, a distinguished looking gentleman in his 60s. Also, Dearborn's city attorney, who was related to a former president of the United States, predicted that the case would be a snap for the city, that the plaintiffs had no chance at all. Joel Underwood was the assistant city attorney.

Judge Neuenfeldt decided that she should not handle the case, and all the other judges on the bench also refused to take it, so a judge – a most eloquent judge – was brought in from Flint. The trial ran every day from 9 a.m. to 5 p.m. with an hour for lunch and lasted for two weeks.

Gallagher really tossed Michael around, but he managed to corner counsel on cross-examination. Gallagher would stand and raise his hand. That would stop Michael, out of deference. He would give the answer in his objections to the witness.

After Gallagher did that a few times, Michael caught on...and as soon as Michael did the same thing to him, Gallagher said, "I'm sick and tired of this, your honor. With all respect, he's testifying instead of letting the witness testify." So that stopped him.

Then Gallagher put a witness on the stand that testified about the speed he traveled on the road and how the claim that the homes rattled was frivolous. The drivers had tested their trucks and even had a seismographic machine and an expert witness, a professor from the University of Michigan, testify in support of the drivers.

By a stroke of good luck, a copy of the professor's findings had landed on Michael's desk, instead of Joel Underwood's. In the professor's testimony in court, he changed the information that was in that document.

The expert witness said, in response to Gallagher's question, "Oh, those were my original results, but you have to divide the numbers by two. You did that, didn't you? That's pretty much it, Mr. Gallagher. "

By the time Michael was finished with this expert witness, he made a monkey out of him. "If you divide the original figures that you gave by two, can you tell me why they don't coincide with these figures?" Michael asked, showing the witness's document that had mysteriously been delivered to him.

The judge became very angry, and by the time Gallagher was finished and the jury was up, he turned to the professor and ordered "Don't you ever come to my courtroom again."

Then Gallagher put the truck drivers on the stand to explain that they could not have created the kind of problem that the plaintiffs were describing. Unbeknownst to Gallagher, Michael had some inside information on one of the trucks, so on cross-examination of one of the drivers, Michael asked, "What did your speedometer indicate?"

The trucker responded with the speed that he thought he was going.

"You're sure that was the speed that you were traveling?" Michael asked.

"Absolutely."

"Let me ask you one other question," Michael continued. "This truck that you were driving was it this dump truck?" (Showing a picture to the witness)

"Oh, yes."

"If I recall correctly that truck doesn't have a speedometer."

"That's right," the driver responded.

"Then how did you figure how fast you were going?"

"I could see the speedometer on the truck in front of me."

It was so ridiculous that the judge started to laugh. After a week, the judge sent an 11-page opinion stating that Michael's findings were correct, that the company violated the zoning ordinance and therefore they were not entitled to proceed with their plans. He gave Michael a permanent injunction.

"As I was reading the judge's findings, Edward C. Levy walked up to me," Michael recalls. "He put his arm around me and said, 'Mike, I guess I hired the wrong lawyer.' What a wonderful person! His son, Edward C. Levy, Jr., and I served together on the Board of Trustees of Children's Hospital years later."

Michael averaged out his hourly rate working for the Homeowners Association for which he became an honorary president. He had earned 93 cents an hour. Many days, he had worked until two or three in the morning and did his own detective work, because he couldn't afford to hire anyone.

The people from the South End were so good to Michael; they virtually idolized him afterwards. It would not be the first time that Michael took a back seat to earnings for the sake of justice. Although Michael eventually left the South End, the South End never left Michael Berry.

"Mike Berry was one of the most distinguished residents in the South End," says Vince Bruno. "He's one of the guys who really did well. Keep in mind anybody that's anybody in Dearborn came out of the South End. He was a pioneer."

Chapter 5

The law firm of Berry, Hopson & Francis would earn a reputation for its effective and expeditious handling of cases primarily in the area of municipal law. The practice would grow to include a battery of partners and employees to serve municipalities, school districts, corporations, and a certain number of small businesses and individuals.

Certain distinctions befell Michael Berry along the way. On February 28, 1950, he was admitted to practice before the Michigan Supreme Court. Seven years later, on May 19, 1958, he was admitted to practice before the United States Supreme Court. Wilber Brucker, a Michigan native and Secretary of the Army under President Dwight D. Eisenhower, arranged for his son and the Dearborn Bar Association members, including Michael Berry to go to Washington, D. C., where they were admitted at the same time.

From 1951 to 1992, the practice was located in Detroit's Cadillac Towers. Forty-eight years later, the firm moved to Warren Avenue in Dearborn, the heart of the largest Arab American community in the United States.

Long before then, the firm had changed its name to Berry, Hopson, Francis, Seifman, Salamey & Harris. Barry Seifman practiced with the firm for 20 years, until 1998, and Sam Salamey came on board in 1987 and stayed until Michael retired in 2000. Laura Berry-Harris, Michael's eldest daughter, earned her law degree from Detroit College of Law in 1987 and was welcomed into her father's practice.

"I've said it before and I've said it in and out of his presence," says Michael, "if I had to have a lawyer, it would be John Francis."

The partners [Michael and John] used to rib Thornton. "His full name was Burdett Thornton Hopson," says John. "We used to laughingly refer to him as the *Americani*, because his family goes all the way back to James Thornton, who signed the Declaration of Independence. So we had a touch of Americana in our firm. We used to tell him, 'Never mind your legal ability; we like your name.'"

Michael Berry, the first Muslim to practice law in Michigan

So, there were two partners – Berry and Hopson. Then, there were three. "We never argued about the order," says John, "although sometimes I questioned it."

The story of how the original three became partners is nothing short of amazing. They started with a handshake, back in the times when that was a gentleman's word, his bond. They never had a written contract in all of the years they practiced law together.

Michael met Thornton Hopson through Vivian's father, who mentioned that Thornton was interested in making a change. One evening, Hopson and his wife, Betty, joined Michael, Vivian and her father for dinner.

"Afterwards," Michael recalls, "Thornton and I retired to the living room and talked for about five minutes, shook hands, and that was it. He became a partner. We commenced the partnership in 1952 with just a handshake, no written documents. We have added to that partnership, at times regretfully, and other times things worked out."

John L. Francis came on the scene in 1955, after returning from service in Korea. By then, Michael was well known in the area for, among other reasons, being the first Muslim attorney to practice in Michigan, something no one else could every lay claim to.

John Francis could have become Michael's first partner. "John came before Thornton," Michael recalls, "but he told me he wanted to think about it before he made up his mind whether or not to join the firm. So, Thornton became my first partner, and then John returned and expressed interest in joining. He became the second partner in the law firm."

Formerly associated with a Jewish attorney by the name of Ben Gans, John told his father, "I'm going to join the firm of Michael Berry and Thornton Hopson and become a partner."

"Well, John, you're going to make up you own mind, but think twice before you leave a Jew to join a Moslem Arab," his father reacted.

That, according to John, was how far back the friction was ingrained. "It certainly turned out wrong between Mike and me, but that's how interesting it was at that time."

The law firm grew by leaps and bounds. They started in a four-office suite of 5,000 square feet and expanded eventually to occupy the entire 20th floor – 10,000 square feet – of the Cadillac Tower.

"We grew on our reputation, not because we had the golden spoon," says John. "Mike's leadership was an important part of it. We used to refer to him as the Rainmaker. Thornton and I could never have achieved the success we did in the practice without Mike giving so much of his time to so many different organizations and charities. He quietly gave, and he gave a lot.

"This was one thing he taught me about Islam. One of the requirements of that faith is to give to charity. We never argued when he wanted

Michael Berry, Cadillac Tower Office, 1960s

to set something up – on behalf of the firm – because there's an old saying that one hand feeds the other. You could see behind the whole thing; there weren't just the three of us. Somebody upstairs was helping us through it all. And we all had bad times, now and then. "

"I first got to know Michael Berry when I was a young prosecutor over 50 years ago," says United States Congressman John Dingell. "Michael was a fine lawyer. He served his people well. He was an honorable practitioner of the law, something which is becoming scarcer today. His word was good. His commitments were honored. We started a friendship that has lasted through the years."

Case highlights

With 50 years of a law practice, it is impossible to recount all of the cases they undertook or even come close, but Michael and John sat down and reminisced for this book. The stories retold here are among their most memorable ones.

John credits some of the firm's success to Michael's willingness to be active in the political arena. "He went 24 hours a day. In fairness to him, every once in a while when Hopson or I would stand in for him in court, the judge would ask, 'Is there a Michael Berry?'

"Mike didn't try a lot of cases, except in the early years. Later on, we would say to him, you go to work and do what you do best, and we'll do what we do best."

At one time, Michael had aspirations to run for judgeship. Selfishly or otherwise, Thornton and John talked him out of it. Eventually, the firm took on municipal representation and over the years represented many communities.

"Thornton or I didn't bring them in. It was Mike's connections with the Democratic Party, his own personal ability, and his lasting friendship with people across the board," John says. "He could meet somebody and instill in that person a lot of respect, first of all, and confidence, because Mike is a forceful kind of man. He can turn it on when he has to or can sit back and let it come to him. "

Many laws are now on the books because of Michael Berry's connections with the legislature. At one point, the firm had done so much municipal work that silk stocking firms – firms that had been around for hundreds of years – were coming to Michael to push for certain legislation. Michael could convince legislators in Lansing of the benefits of a certain type of law that he promoted.

Riverview

Before Michael became involved in county politics or the Wayne County Road Commission, a situation arose in which John researched the law and found a seldom-used segment of the law. The firm was representing Riverview that has frontage on the Detroit River.

The city had tried to get the people to vote for a bond that would allow them to take a Huntington drain and cover it. "We don't think of that today," notes John, "but there used to be open drains all over the area that carried water and sewage and dumped it into the river."

The state and federal governments started to tell municipalities they had to do something about it to clean up the problem. The city couldn't get the votes, so as the city's attorneys, Berry, Hopson & Francis was asked about how to proceed.

The firm suggested that a law that permitted "court-ordered bonds" needed no votes, but in the general welfare of the community, the court could order the bond money to repair the problem.

"See, there had been five or six cases of hepatitis from that open-drain situation," explains John. "On the strength of that – somehow, some way – the citizens started a lawsuit. The state health department – somehow, some way – got wind of that and brought a suit, ordering Riverview to clean up the situation.

"The judge said, 'Well, why don't you clean it up?' We explained that we would like to but couldn't, so he ordered the bond. We had the money to do it, and of course it's all paid for and gone now, but we were the first community to put into practice that little-used law, and it's been used over and over since then."

An offshoot of this story was a trip that the firm took in the early 1960s. At that time, Wayne County had a master plan to put together all of the Downriver communities that did not have a waterfront – Taylor, Allen Park, Lincoln Park, and others. The goal was to create a master sewer division, one sewer to run the storm water and the other to run the sanitary, which was not a big deal.

"The sewers were all combined at one time, but they had to separate them, the one water being more polluted than the other, and they wanted to treat that water," John explains. "Well, they wanted to treat the water on the water's edge, because then the tributary goes out into the river or wherever after it's purified, because you have to get rid of it.

"Well, Riverview was right on the river, and it was a small community of less than 10,000 people. The city fathers said that to get into the county system would cost them a certain amount, but why did they have to get into that system when they could do it themselves."

It was necessary to float a bond to get enough money to handle this problem. There were only two silk stocking firms in Michigan that would pass on the legality of the bond. According to John, before they could get the money, New York bankers or big financiers would buy the bond. To get that, they wanted a legal opinion from a law firm that it was legal and could not be challenged.

Michael and John went to the two Michigan firms and found that neither could represent them, due to conflict of interest. Bill Hettinger, a municipal consultant, told them about a law firm in Chicago that bonded the entire western half of the country. He set up an appointment for them. They went to Chicago, with Michael's cousin Harry driving them.

So, there were four of them, and John was familiar with Chicago, so they had a great time. The firm, Cutler & Cutler, was located in down-town Chicago in not one, but two buildings, each 30 or 40 stories high with a bridge connecting them. There they arrived, two sons of immigrants and one guy out of the back hills of Missouri.

They were greeted by a short gentleman and ushered into a magnificent office to wait. A short while later, the same man returned with five other men who represented cities across the country.

"Gentlemen, how can we help you?" the man said in a British accent. He was wearing an English tweed suit that, Michael recalls, if he had taken the suit off, it would have stood on its own, that's how heavy and thick it was.

"We would like to have your firm represent us," Michael said. They had peanuts, and there they were, talking to a firm that makes a million and a half, two million. But, if they were to sign the bond, everyone would buy it because of the firm's reputation.

"Why do you come to me?" the man asked. "You have a couple of firms in Michigan that can handle this for you."

Michael explained that, due to conflict of interest, neither of those firms would take the case. Finally, the gentleman said, "We'll give you whatever you want. In fact, I'll tell you what we'll do. You give us this bond issue and we'll make you our agent for the State of Michigan to direct all of that business to us, and we'll undersell and underwrite their fees, and we'll get you whatever you want."

Underscoring this offer was a lingering angry feeling of this man towards Nunnelly, one of the Michigan law firms, which had run him out of Michigan years earlier. This was his chance to get even. "You go back and tell your people…" he said.

Michael and John went back to Riverview all excited. "The net result," Michael explains, "was that they caved in and sought to bring pressure against the city administration, which they were capable of doing. There is a lot of give and take in politics, and we were prevailed upon to listen to what local bond firms had to offer and we did. That's when we told them that they weren't the only ones who could do business in the State of Michigan."

The firm gained a lot of respect from the way they handled this problem, and they ultimately succeeded. They were the so-called experts in municipal law at that time. The firm had an AV rating, which was the highest rating a firm could get.

"We took on Miller-Canfield's office and accepted Strat Brown as the person to do business with instead of Nunnelly, out of deference to the gentleman from Chicago," Michael relates. "So Strat Brown handled the bond issue, and he was an excellent man, a fine person. We worked well together.

"But even to that point in time, they felt not only our presence but also they should do something to dull the effect of our presence. They went to the person who used to be with the attorney general's office who passed on fees, and apparently they put enough pressure on that aspect of it for him to review what our fees were. And our fees were nominal. He was threatening to knock our fees far below the minimum that was tolerated by any law firm, let alone experts in the field of municipal law, like we were."

So, the only dispute that landed the firm on the front page of the local newspapers was over their fee, which was $19,000 for the three years it took to achieve successful resolution. They never billed the city a single penny and paid all incurred costs and expenses, such as the trip to Chicago, out of their own pockets.

The Municipal Finance Commission, which was behind the dispute, decided to go to every community that Berry, Hopson & Francis represented and ask them what they thought of the firm.

"If memory serves me correctly," said Michael, "they went to Garden City, and the mayor at the time – God rest his soul – said, 'They are worth their weight in gold.' He was quoted in the paper."

Garden City

In another section, we explore Michael's involvement in politics, but it was his involvement with the 16th Democratic Congressional District that drew the attention of the city clerk from Garden City. He visited Berry, Hopson & Francis one day to talk about the firm serving as attorney for the city. His main concern was that the city had three cases in the Supreme Court and the city needed a firm that was more involved to handle those cases.

When Michael said they would serve as city attorney for Garden City, the man who had been serving in that capacity became quite upset. He was involved in litigation with certain developers on pay back agreements, and the case was pending in circuit court before Judge Baum.

Garden City, at the time, had a lot of problems. One of the city attorneys got shot...the mayor got shot...and so on. So, the firm started serving the city, knowing they could not beat the case. John even told the city that the case was a loser, and Michael concurred.

The city persevered, saying that if they didn't get into that case, they would lose more on the next case. They pleaded with the firm to do something with the first case to help the other cases. And so they did. They argued a certain part of the law – it's actually in the books as Smith v Garden City. But the judge ruled against them.

Despite losing that first case, the firm served as city attorneys for Garden City for 31 years. First, there was legal representation of the townships of Romulus, Dearborn, Van Buren, and Huron, and the cities of Riverview, Dearborn Heights, Woodhaven, and Romulus. There were a few times that the City of Dearborn called on Michael for legal counsel, as well.

Public Administrator

Michael encountered an unpleasant experience in the 1960s when Neil Staebler controlled the Democratic Party; ultimately, he became a congressman-at-large. This experience happened because of Michael's friendship with his very first law partner, Carl Weideman, son of Judge Carl Weideman, Sr. "As a circuit court judge, he had encountered a man by the name of Ted Souris, who became a Supreme Court justice and married into the Chrysler hierarchy. Souris was very close to Staebler," says Michael.

"As I was told, Ted Souris appeared before Judge Weideman, who, during the trial, really dressed him down. Now, that's on information; I wasn't there, so I really don't know what transpired. I do know that there was hatred between Souris and the Weidemans. I think that translated into Staebler's office, and I was a friend of Carl's, so by the process of osmosis, I received that same ill feeling.

"When it came time for the appointment of public administrator, my name was submitted, along with another from our district who was far lower on the totem pole than I was, and he got the appointment.

"A few months later, my name was submitted again when there was another vacancy, and again I was overlooked. I went to the UAW and told them what was happening and that I couldn't understand why I was being overlooked. I had not been elected chairman of the district yet, but I was on the executive committee at that time."

The UAW told Michael to call Staebler and make an appointment to find out what was behind this oversight. He did, and when Michael went for the appointment, Staebler made him wait an hour and a half. Finally his turn came.

"By this time, I was really hot under the collar, and I didn't give a damn who he was or what he was. I said, 'I'd like to know what's really going on. Here I've been working for the Democratic Party all these years, and the first appointment I get, I'm shunted aside. The second one, I'm shunted aside. I'd like to know what's happening.'"

Staebler responded, "Well, your record has been red-lined."

"For what reason?" Michael questioned.

"Well, our sounding board in Wayne County say you've got a skeleton in your closet," Staebler explained. [According to Michael, Ted Souris was the only person who could have been the sounding board.]

"Well, let me tell you this," said Michael. "If I'm not appointed, I want you to come out and tell the press about the skeleton in my closet. I want you to identify it, and if you don't, I'm going to go to the press and tell them why you are not appointing me and that you have accused me of having a skeleton in my closet." He walked out.

He received a call from labor. "Mike, we've asked Staebler to come and tell the 16th District why he hasn't appointed you."

Staebler stood before the group and delivered a mealy-mouth, wishy-washy statement that the time was not right for Michael to be public administrator and so on, with no mention of a skeleton in his closet.

Michael then rose to the occasion, and he was hot. "I delivered the toughest speech I ever gave and received a standing ovation. They literally booed Staebler out of the district."

When the next public administrator post became available, Attorney General Thomas Kavanaugh appointed Michael to serve. "That just meant more legal business," notes Michael, "but at least I didn't let Staebler get away with it. Years later, when I was district chairman and Staebler wanted to be congressman, he came to me hat in hand, asking for my support. I looked at him and told myself not to be like him.

"After he finished speaking, I said, 'You know, in spite of all the ill feelings I have toward you, I'll still support you.' And that was that."

Sometimes standing your own ground means having to give a little in the long run, but you can hold your head up, knowing you have not allowed someone to stand in your path to success and destiny fulfillment.

Notable PA cases

The public administrator is the person called in by the probate courts when someone dies with no heirs. The public administrator's duty is to preserve the assets of the deceased and search for heirs.

Michael eventually turned his public administrator duties over to Thornton Hopson. In that capacity, several interesting cases arose. One, in particular, taught a great lesson.

Usually whoever found the dead person called the police, they would investigate and then call the PA's office, then seal the apartment or house to preserve whatever assets were there. So the firm had a connection with the local police, generally.

Thornton received a telephone call that a couple had been found dead. Hopson went to their beautiful apartment and returned to the office in tears.

"You know, guys, you don't realize what I ran into today. I walked in there. The police were already on the scene. All over the apartment was paper money, thrown all over the apartment in every room. I picked up all the money and counted it. The police were assisting in the count, so no one could put any in their pockets.

"This man, retired and in his 80s, had done very well for himself and his wife. He had cared for his wife all the years she suffered from cancer.

Evidently she passed away in the night, and he killed himself, because he couldn't stand living alone. In that last moment, he took whatever he thought were the riches that didn't mean a thing to him anymore and, in vented anger, threw that money all over the apartment."

John relates that story as one that always impressed him and the other partners in the firm. "The old man realized that all his money didn't buy him the happiness he thought he would have, and then his wife died, and they had no children. All of the man's assets, including the cash, were accounted for and turned over to the public administrator."

A lot of people say that if you die, the state gets your money, John explains. "That is true, but anyone can come forward forever and prove that they're entitled to it, and they get paid. The state figures, however, that they might as well use the money and earn interest off of it instead of leaving it in a bank."

That's where the escheat law comes in, which governs forfeiture of property (including bank accounts) to the state treasury if it appears certain that there are no heirs, descendants or named beneficiaries to take the property upon the death of the last known owner.

"We had a lot of chances to make money," John continues. "A lot of chances that were border line and we never hesitated, because we understood each other's honesty. I mean, we understood it. God bless us; we used to be attacked left and right, people saying how we were making out so well with our law practice. We were investigated, cross-examined, and everything else, several times."

Their honesty, integrity, and high standards always prevailed, and they were indeed blessed abundantly.

Austin High School

At the time this case arose, Michael, a Ford Motor Company veteran who had worked on the line and was a member of UAW Local 600, received a telephone call from the president of the local about his son, a top-notch quarterback at Austin High School. Sports programs were very strong in those days, and Austin had a great football program.

"One of the rules was that you could begin practice only on August 15th, not before," says John. "Well, the coach had taken the team over to Canada and allegedly they practiced before August 15th, although they claimed they did not wear their uniforms. They were reported to the CYO and suspended for the whole year. The kids could play football, but they could not be champions. This greatly affected the kids' ability to get football scholarships. The local president told me it wasn't fair. I told him we would do what we could."

John couldn't convince the judge that the court had any authority over the archdiocese. The firm lost the case, but they had tried, and some of the kids received scholarships anyway, so they did help.

For the partners of Michael Berry's law firm, the importance wasn't in winning but in doing their best. Indeed, they did, often being willing to reach into their own pockets to make right a wrong.

Children's Hospital

An immigrant, who worked in a bakery for three or four dollars an hour, went to Michael and said his four-year-old son needed eye surgery. The man's story and financial limitations touched Michael, who served on the Board of Trustees of Children's Hospital.

Michael called the hospital and talked to Tom Rozak, who was then the assistant administrator. "I told him the story and that whatever the cost of the surgery amounted to, the firm would pick up the tab, but he told me, 'No that's not the way we handle things. Let's see if he qualifies for indigent care. We'll take care of him.'

"I called the father and told him to take his son to Children's Hospital. As a result, doctors operated successfully on the boy, and he sees well today."

This was in the 1980s. Michael happened into a discussion at the mosque with a man who told Michael that he was not doing enough for the community. Michael questioned him on the definition of "enough."

After the immigrant's son had recovered from eye surgery, Michael called the man at the mosque. "I reminded him what he said and suggested, 'Why don't you talk to the father of this boy and hear for yourself whether I have been doing enough.' What he was asking me to do was free immigration work, which I refused to do. There were immigration law firms, but we were not one of them."

Strict adherence to principle became the cornerstone of Michael Berry's work in all aspects of his life – law, politics, community service, and charity.

Overseas rescue mission

John likes to tell the story of a troubled man from the Bloomfield Hills area whose daughter was overseas. He contacted Michael, although he knew nothing of him, but had been referred. There was an air of urgency about the man and his need to see Michael quickly. Michael set up an appointment that afternoon.

"When we had someone come in like that, we got into the habit, having been attacked by people who wanted to get even for jealousy or whatever reason, of having one of the other partners sit in on the first appointment," John explains. "We never knew what that person was after."

The gentleman came into the office and said, "Mr. Berry, I've come to you because I've talked to the U. S. State Department, and they can't do anything for me. I've talked to my congressman and he can't help me. And your name came up as someone who might be able to help."

"I will if I can," Michael replied. "What is it?"

The man explained that his daughter, who was a student at the University of Michigan, became involved with a dope head, and the father lost control of her. She went with this fellow to Europe, and in their travels ended up in Syria, where authorities found marijuana or some kind of drugs on her young traveling companion. They both went to jail and were still in jail. Suddenly, the girl realized how much she needed her father, so she tried to contact him. Again, this was in the early 1980s, and when the man went to the State Department, they told him that the United States has no Embassy in Syria, so they could not help him.

"Well," said Michael, "very frankly, I don't know if I can help you, but I will try."

Now, according to John, there was no discussion at that time about fees or how much the rescue of this man's daughter was worth to him. Strictly out of Michael's own good heart, he called a relative in Lebanon, who told him he would investigate for Michael.

They waited about a week and finally received a call from Lebanon. "We need a paid ticket with TWA and a deposit of a certain amount in a bank in Lebanon," the relative said. Michael recalls that it cost $10,000 to hire someone in Syria to handle the case.

Michael told the father, "Honestly, this could be the biggest fraud in the world. You might lose the money you're going to deposit in that bank."

"Look," the man replied, "I have nowhere else to turn." The daughter was home in two days.

"What they did," John tells, "is they took the money and whatever they did with it, they got her out on bond, which you never hear of, because they have no habeas corpus in Syria. They don't have to try you right away; they can let you rot in prison until you die before they even bring you to trial. But they smuggled her across the border into Lebanon, put her on a TWA flight, and told her one thing: Don't ever come back.

"In fairness to Mike and everyone else, this man would have given Mike the world for what he did. The story was never publicized."

AWOL

In another story that shows Michael Berry's goodhearted nature, a distraught man had gone AWOL in the service during training leading up to World War II. His records were about 40 years old at the time in the 1980s, when this story came to light at the firm.

He had lived in fear since then, always looking over his shoulder, expecting that the FBI was looking for him. The man had grown up and had five kids and was a success in his business. He still lived every day, worried that he might get arrested for what he had done some 40 years earlier.

He called Michael and told him, "If only I could find out, it would put my mind at ease."

Michael made a call and learned that the man's case – among perhaps hundreds or thousands of other cases – had been closed. Imagine the relief that man felt just being told that no one was looking for him anymore.

"We never met the man," said John. "He came to us through an attorney friend of mine." Those are some of the things Mike did in his time as a result of his position.

"Not for wealth," says John, "not for money, because that came on the side. You know they say, you cast your bread on the water, it comes back somehow, somewhere else. We were firm believers of that."

Chapter 6

International recognition

In 1963, Michael Berry was chosen as the first-generation American to be depicted in material circulated overseas as to what someone from another cultural background can accomplish in this country. The *Detroit Free Press*, identifying the Berry family as "the typical American family", devoted an entire section to him, his family, and his many accomplishments.

"After the article appeared in the newspaper, the United States Information Agency (USIA) in Washington, D.C. contacted me and made arrangements for me to meet there with John Dingell, my congressman," Michael relates. "So John Francis and I went to Washington, and we talked." President Eisenhower had created the USIA in 1953 to promote public diplomacy. The agency wanted Michael to travel to Egypt and Lebanon as a non-paid grantee of the USIA on a mission of goodwill and give speeches as to what America was like and how it treated its immigrants.

In April 1966 Michael began his journey with a five-week tour of Lebanon. Along with him went Vivian, daughters Gail, Carol, and Cindi [Laura was married then and preferred to stay at home], his brother Jim and his wife, and a couple of other people, who knew that Michael would be received by dignitaries in Lebanon and wanted to tag along. "One of them was Sam Mallad, the father of Suzanne Sareini, Dearborn city councilwoman, who held himself out as my secretary."

Not having been in Lebanon for 36 years, Michael's impression was the same as when he left as a young boy, although he had heard much about how modernized Lebanon had become and had seen pictures of hotels and other buildings in Beirut. He knew that things had changed, and all to the good. The infrastructure – roads, the airport, and so on – was more modern.

"When we landed at the airport, there was a delegation from the

L to R: Congressman John Dingell, his secretary, Michael Berry, John L. Francis, Washington, D. C., 1966

Lebanese government waiting to greet us. Apparently they had been put on notice by the USIA. We were greeted by a number of dignitaries, even from the president's office and from members of Parliament, and by my cousin, Nabih Berri, who is currently president of Parliament, but he was an attorney then. In order to keep peace among the many important people that wanted to transport us into the city, I put different members of my family in different cars.

"We had made reservations at the fashionable Phoenicia Hotel, the newest hotel in downtown Beirut, overlooking the Mediterranean. The Inter-Continental Hotel chain had opened it just five years earlier; it was the company's first hotel outside of the western hemisphere.

"We stayed at the Phoenicia the entire five weeks that we were in Lebanon. Beirut, then considered the Paris of the Middle East, was simply gorgeous! One of the things that I remember to this day and I can picture it right now was one night sitting on the balcony with Vivian. As we looked out to the Mediterranean, we saw a United States aircraft carrier, all lit up. What a sight that was! When you see something like that, a feeling of pride wells up inside of you, as if you were the owner of it. It was you; you were a part of it. It was so magnificent a sight, I cannot tell you. And I cannot express the degree of pride I had in witnessing this example of Americanism. Vivian and I stayed up watching it and other sights until the very early hours of the next morning."

Guides assigned to take Michael to meetings and other functions often showed up in the hotel lobby as early as 6 a.m. They had planned a rather hectic agenda for his stay in Lebanon, and it seemed they wanted to waste no time. Shortly after Michael and his family arrived in Beirut, a gathering of 500 businessmen met at the trendy Yildizlar Restaurant.

"I had a tremendous headache, perhaps from jet lag. I was sitting next to a man, and he asked what my problem was. I explained that I had such a splitting headache that I felt I could not participate in the function. So the man left. I found out later that he was a druggist, and he went to his drugstore, opened it up at night, and got some medicinal powder. He returned to the restaurant and told me to mix it in some water and drink it, which I did. It relieved my headache to some degree, as least enough so I could participate in the function. That was my first introduction to Lebanese hospitality. Everywhere I went, it was 'He's an American.' Then you take great pride in the fact that you are an American, not like today when you go overseas and almost have to hide your identity. I tell you; it was wonderful back then."

Michael's first cousin, Lila Berry, remembers that trip in 1966. "By the time he arrived in Lebanon, he was already recognized. The people there didn't take him as a Berry; they took him as a Lebanese. They respected him as a Lebanese, who was getting ahead in the United States. At that time, he was rare. Lebanese didn't have that kind of success in those days in America. Most of the Lebanese there were immigrants and were barely making it. Michael became a role model for the younger generations who would go to America. They took his example that they didn't have to just work in a factory; they could become professionals."

Michael spoke at the Palace of Justice and before the Lebanese Bar Association. He also met with three members of the Supreme Court of Lebanon. "To some degree, these lawyers and judges wanted to know about the law practice in America, but for the most part it wasn't a vital topic of conversation. Most of them were interested in what life was like in America, and I think about 90 percent of them wished that they were practicing law in the United States."

"When Michael addressed them, it was attorney to attorney," relates John Francis. "It was an indication of the ability of this man and the American system to rise to that position. He lectured them and answered their questions. We're proud of him. He earned it. He didn't have to pull any shenanigans to get that assignment, either. He lived his life, practiced his faith, and did what he thought was right. He kept honest, which is not always easy to do in this business when people come at you with all kinds of problems, to gain your favor."

One member of a Lebanese Court of Appeals, who was born and raised in Tibnin, made arrangements to spend some one-on-one time with Michael. "The following morning at 7 a. m., he took me to an Austrian woman's breakfast shop. There we chose from a delectable selection of Austrian and German pastries and, of course, coffee. We sat there overlooking the Mediterranean and talking in Arabic for about two hours. As it turned out, I had known his sister when I was a child; then, she was a grown married woman living in Highland Park."

Michael spent considerable time with his cousin, Nabih Berri, who escorted him to meetings and on sightseeing side trips. "Nabih is a very brilliant man, who had done great things for Lebanon, such as improving the living conditions in South Lebanon. He brought water and electricity into the villages, and he modernized the roads in the south. In the past, the so-called elitists of South Lebanon were interested only in how much money they made. Nabih was a different sort of person. He is a great patriot. The people in South Lebanon swear by him. He has held office for a number of years, most recently as speaker or president of Parliament, and he'll be there for a long time. He's a truly remarkable, charismatic person.

"His son, Abdullah is a very bright young man, too. He had done great work for the poor people in Tibnin, establishing a large orphanage there and contributing a great deal toward improving the educational facilities in the village."

In addition to the many parties held in Michael's honor during his five-week stay in Lebanon, his cousin Lila remembers when they all went to Casino du Liban, a beautiful place that hosted great shows from all over the world. "Vivian told me that she had seen many shows in Las Vegas and other places, but they were nothing compared to this one in Beirut."

When Michael was at meetings and other functions during the day,

L to R: Michael Berry, Nabih Berri and Lila Berry at Casino du Liban, Beirut, 1966

Vivian and the girls lived it up on their own! They would sit by the pool at the Phoenicia and play the role of visiting royalty, summoning waiters to bring Cokes and food; they waited on them hand and foot. Michael drove them to Tibnin, just to the village and back, but the girls were able to see where their grandparents were born. "What a wonderful time we had!"

The beauty of Beirut was dazzling, and the hospitality of its people heartwarming, but neither tempted Michael to give up his life in America. "Well, I could live there, but I would not. I guess the American spirit is too well grounded in me that there is no other country I could call home. I love my heritage; there is no question about that, but there is also no place like home. For me, home is the United States of America."

After five weeks in Lebanon, it was time to fulfill the remainder of his USIA mission by traveling to Egypt. "I visited the ambassador there and talked to a group of Egyptian lawyers. I was in Egypt only about 10 days, and I spent at least three of those days at the National Museum, which totally fascinated me. One could spend 30 days there alone and not see everything. It is unbelievable what the Egyptians did 5,500 years ago. They must have been a brilliant race to have achieved so many amazing things."

[The Egyptian Museum in Cairo, established in 1835, houses over 120,000 collections, including mummies, sarcophagi, sculpture, and artifacts.]

"At the time I was in Egypt and during my frequent visits to this great museum, they were moving many artifacts, sarcophagi, and other items to the Valley of the Kings, some 400 miles south of Cairo. I regretted that I did not have two extra days needed to make that trip. I would have loved to have seen the Valley of the Kings."

In Cairo, Michael and his family stayed that the Nile Hilton, a 500-room hotel opened in 1959 and overlooking the Nile River. "The hotel was relatively poor compared to the luxurious Phoenicia in Beirut, but the location was great. I went up and down the Nile in one of their boats. At one point, I started to put my hand in the water, but the guide cautioned me, 'Don't do that. The Nile is a filthy river.' So I refrained.

The family found time to enjoy some of the normal tourist sites. "We went to Tent City on the outskirts of Cairo, and there we saw the nightclubs under the colorful, intricately woven tents, and that was exciting. [Today the Tent City, known as "Fostat" in ancient times, is called "Old Cairo" or "Misr Al Kadima", where one finds the Citadel and some old, famous mosques.]

"We rode in cars to the Great Sphinx of Giza, the monumental statue that is part man, part lion. We all rode camels and visited one of the pyramids. [Perhaps it was the Great Pyramid of Khufu, the largest in Egypt, located on the Giza Plateau in full view of the Sphinx.]

"When we entered the tomb, we had to stoop. Now, I'm not a tall guy, so I asked the guide, 'Why is the ceiling so low?' He replied, 'You've got to understand; 5,000 years ago, people were not tall. They were shorter than we are today.'

"When they built the stairway that wound its way to the top, they had a space so many inches wide alongside the staircase. It was a flat surface made of cement that went all the way around, and every so often there were holes. I asked the guide about the significance of the holes. 'In those days, when they wanted to bring the sarcophagus up to its resting place, they would lay it on the slab, and then the men would push it up. Whenever they needed to rest, they would put a pole in one of the holes to brace the weighty sarcophagus. After they caught their breath a bit, they would move the stone coffin container to the next hole. They did that all the way to the top.'"

When the group reached the top of the pyramid, the guide said, "You notice that it's cooler up here." Knowing that heat rises and that this cooling defies the law of physics, Michael said, "Yes, you are right. It is cooler up here, when it should be hotter. How is that?"

"The engineers back 5,500 years had their own method of air conditioning," explained the guide. "They channeled the outside air in such as way so that when it came through and circulated, it cooled off the upper level."

The USIA trip to Lebanon and Egypt was a great success. It marked not only a time when Michael found special recognition and reception in his parents' homeland, but also a time when he deepened his ties to his own homeland of America. He made a lasting impression on the people of Lebanon, one that touched lives long after he had left.

Lebanon Welcomes Attorney General Frank Kelley

Michigan's former Attorney General Frank Kelley recalls a time when he personally felt the effect of Michael's international reputation. "Leading up to my U. S. Senate race in 1972, I made a world tour in late 1971. On that tour was scheduled a three-day visit to Lebanon, which at the time, was the Switzerland of the Middle East. It was a depository of money; it had a banking reputation in the Arab World as the place for economic security and banking stability. That was before the Palestinian refugee influx and the war that followed.

"The stories of Mike and his influence in Detroit had spread back to the entire Lebanese community in Beirut; he was well known there in the 1970s, so much so that when I arrived at the Beirut Airport with my entourage, the plane landed and stopped halfway on the runway before it went to the terminal. The door to the plane opened and the Mayor of Beirut and some other high officials came in. They asked if Mr. Frank Kelley was aboard.

"Of course, I was, as was my staff. They greeted us and escorted us off the plane and put us in a limousine and drove us to the VIP lounge at the edge of the airport. There, we saw a big sign, WELCOME MICHIGAN'S ATTORNEY GENERAL FRANK KELLEY TO

LEBANON. A band played, and at least a dozen public officials were on hand to meet us.

"All of this was arranged by Mike Berry with one phone call. It was the best reception I received on my entire tour of Europe and the Middle East. That was the type of influence and respect that Mike carried in Beirut, and not only with Muslims, but with Christians as well.

"My personal escort during my stay in Lebanon was the son of a former president whose older brother later became president of Lebanon. He was killed, and the one who escorted me subsequently became president of Lebanon. Out of respect for Mike, his family made sure someone in the family was with me at all times. I was entertained one night by the Christian Lebanese, and one night by Muslim Lebanese, and each would outdo the other with their hospitality and generosity. This was all because I was Mike Berry's friend."

Chapter 7

Workers Compensation cases – UAW Locals

UAW Local 600 became one of Michael's long-term clients, serving 30 years as legal counsel to its members. The Local, which grew out of the Hunger March and Battle of the Overpass, at its peak had more than 100,000 members and retired workers.

"He did the legal work concerning benefits for people coming out of the Ford foundry," recalls Vince Bruno. "The company agreed they were liable to contract emphysema or silicosis, and Mike took up the cases for us. He also represented retired workers or those who had been injured on the job. On the last day of each month, Mike would come to Local 600 and meet with all the retired workers and advise them."

Although John Francis often handled the Workers Compensation cases, most of the people were Michael's clients out of UAW Local 600 or one of the other UAW locals that the firm represented.

"Workers Compensation is a Michigan law that says if you are hurt or disabled on a job, you are entitled to so much money," John explains. "We had cases that came out of the power house, the foundry, at Ford Motor Company, those areas where workers breathe that dust for 40 years and end up with emphysema, silicosis, dirt on their lungs, and so forth."

They interviewed a number of those men, and some of the stories were very interesting. They were older men; so basically, they were giving the history of Ford Motor Company. Some of the stories are still fresh in John's memory, and although most of them came to John, they all came to the firm, thanks to Michael Berry.

A German named Hans

One was about Hans, a young German, who started at Ford when he was 16. He was a cabinetmaker. At the age of 65 or 66, he was working one day and all of a sudden he heard all of his stock getting knocked around. He turned around, and there was old Henry Ford himself.

"Now, listen," Ford chastised, "when you work for the Ford Motor Company, you work neatly. You pile this lumber so nobody trips on it and gets hurt. I don't want you messing this area." Then Ford said, "Wait a minute. This is mahogany. What are you working on with mahogany?"

Now, the carpenters at Ford used to make the wood doors and woody wagons; Ford had a plant up in northern Michigan that cut the trees and brought the lumber back. The old German didn't speak English well; so he took the plans he was working on and showed them to Ford. He was building the kitchen cabinets for Ford Fairlane, Henry Ford's home.

"Okay, go ahead," Ford said.

It was unlikely that Ford knew his own people were building things for the house on his time, but he could do anything.

Another time Henry Ford went to the carpentry area and said, "Hans, what do you got in your lunch bucket?"

"A knockwurst sandwich and a dill pickle," Hans replied. "You know, Hans," said Ford, "I'd give half of this company if I could eat that sandwich."

By then, Ford had a stomach problem and was probably eating baby Pablum. He couldn't eat a decent meal, but he and this old German were sitting there talking like buddies.

A spark of genius

Another Ford retiree explained to John how he used to wind what they called magnetos. Automobile starters and sparks were not in the old days what they are today. They had to spark the magneto before they could start the car.

To make a magneto, the worker had to take a T-core and wind one side with a certain thickness of wire and the other side with a thinner wire. Then, he would wind it again.

Henry Ford came to him one day and said, "Well, how's it going?"

"Well, Mr. Ford [they never called him Henry], you know you're losing money here."

"What do you mean, I'm losing money?"

"Well, you know, I'm wrapping this with #2 wire and then I come back and I wrap #6 wire four times, and then I wrap #8 wire eight times.

Now, if you wound them all with the #8 wire, you could get the same effect."

"Write that down for me," Ford said. "I'm going to take it up to the slick-wigs (or whatever he used to call the engineers)."

Ford came back a month later and said, "You're absolutely right. Your theory was absolutely true, but not only that, you get a three-cents/hour raise."

That raise made that man the highest paid worker at the plant. A great story.

Citizenship

One Ford retiree of Italian descent came to John, who congratulated him on putting in 40 to 50 years. The man meekly said, "Yes, yes."

"What's the matter?" John asked. "Have you ever gone back to Italy?"

"You know, my church is going to make a trip to my hometown but I can't go," the man said sadly.

"Why?" asked John.

"Well, I'm not sure I'm a citizen," the man said.

"How long have you been in this country?"

"I was brought over here when I was two years old," he said. "My dad came over first. He worked in the UP cutting lumber. They used to line the men up and walk them over to circuit court, because they didn't have a federal court. They'd swear them in as citizens and tell them, now when it's time to vote, you vote for so and so. And they went along with that."

"Well, he could have made you a citizen, if he included your name," John said. "How about your mother?"

"Oh, no," the man said.

John talked to Michael, who told him, "Check on it, John. I'm not talking about taking a fee or anything. Just check on it."

John wrote to the clerk at the county in the UP and asked the clerk to check when the man's mother immigrated and find out if there is a certificate up there. He enclosed five or 10 dollars, whatever the cost for copying the order, if it was there.

In a week, John received the order, declaring Luigi, the father, a citizen as well as his wife and two boys, including the man who came to him.

John called the retiree and told him to come to the office, that he had something for him.

"Here is your citizenship," he told the man, handing him the papers.

The man broke down and cried right there in John's office.

"What's the matter?" John asked.

"This is wonderful, but…"

"Why don't you go on the trip now?"

"It's going to leave in two weeks, and I don't have a passport or visa."

John walked him over to the post office in Detroit and got a waiver. In two days, the man had his passport.

He went to Italy and was gone a month. When he returned, he called John. "I want to take you to lunch. How much do I owe you?"

"God bless you," John said.

"Go ahead and do it," Michael told him.

"We both recognized this first generation," says John, "the fear our people lived under, whether they were here legally or not. We went to lunch, and he handed me a package. This is for your wife."

When John returned home that night, his wife opened the package. It was a beautiful handmade tablecloth made by nuns in Italy. It fit John's dining room table perfectly, and his wife put it out every holiday.

"Isn't that something? The law – if you practice it right – gives you a lot of opportunities," John says.

The practice thrived over the years, doing mostly municipal work, but some bond work and ordinances for various cities and townships. They also did some probate work, but generally, the firm was known for its specialty in municipal law.

Setting new precedence

Barry Seifman joined the law firm early in 1973. "I met Mike through negotiations on an accident case when I was with an insurance company. He said to me, 'You sound very lawyer-y.' I told him that I was going to law school. After the numbers were agreed upon, because Mike is first class ethically, he said, 'Stop and see me when you're done.'

"So, after I graduated magna cum laude from law school at Wayne State in 1972, I had a few different things I could do. One was joining a large law firm. At the second interview they told me what I would be doing for the next 20 years. They thought they were giving me security; I thought it was stifling.

"I then talked to Mike. He made me an offer before I took the Bar exam. I started handling all the personal injury matters. I was making less money than before I graduated, which was 20 dollars an hour. I took the Bar in May and passed it the first time. I was making less money, but I was getting a percentage. Mike said, 'You'll find you'll do better as long as you work here.' He was right. As the years went by, I was making more in that system not being a partner than I would have made as a partner."

The partners sat down with Barry and offered him partnership.

"I won't pay," said Barry.

"What do you mean, you won't pay?" they asked.

"I just don't believe in it," Barry asserted.

So they made Barry a partner without having to pay. "I started a horrible precedent, because no one had to pay after me. I was with Mike for 25 years, and I ended up being the managing partner of the firm."

Sitting in for Michael

"Mike is just a wonderful, unique person, and he's Muslim," says Barry. "Thornton Hopson, his first partner, was Anglo-Saxon Protestant, and John Francis is actually Syrian Catholic. And, of course, I'm Jewish. Those ought to be feuding factions, but we never had a problem. All of us were very sensitive to each other."

One of Barry's favorite stories was when he was the youngest partner in the firm. "Mike used to send me out as a young guy in his place, because there are just so many social things you can attend without getting burned out. One night, he sent me to the Arab-Jewish Friends dinner. This was held in the old American Chaldean Club in Southfield.

"I was sitting in for Mike. Next to me was a guy named Sala and another guy named Faraj, I think. I didn't realize this until we got into it because I recognized a couple of our clients there. Well, Sala was Jewish. Faraj was Christian. And I was supposed to be the Muslim. I was the Muslim-of-the-Day."

Michael was on very good terms with Republican Governor William Milliken, who at times would call Michael in to help negotiate certain union situations. Well, before people recognized Barry, Michael would send him to Republican functions. "And I'm a lifelong Democrat!" Barry says.

Setting a style

According to Barry, people either love Michael or hate him. He's that kind of person. "I remember going with him to Recorders Court. Now, when I started with the firm, Mike was no longer trying cases, so he probably hadn't been in that court for 10 years. There wasn't a person he passed, be it a filing clerk or a bailiff – the people most others ignored – that he didn't say, 'Hi, I'm Michael Berry.' You know, Denny Crane [of ABC's "Boston Legal."]. He was way in front of Denny. Mike would hand out cards. He taught me that.

"Once, when I went into a carry-out restaurant near my house, I said to the owner, 'You know something. I could afford to buy more of your food if you actually sent me some of your legal business.' The owner said, 'I need a lawyer.' And I became his attorney. That's Mike's thing! I learned that from Mike. Socialize. Promote. Do the right thing."

Eventually Laura Berry and Sam Salamey joined the firm. Barry left the firm in 1998, shortly before his 51st birthday, and not long before the firm closed its doors.

Michael Berry, John Francis, and their partners throughout the life of their law firm believed in putting people first. Their financial rewards were great, but in proper perspective, their riches far exceeded those of a monetary nature. They were ambassadors of good will, and their sterling reputation was founded on a firm foundation of integrity, loyalty, and charity.

Legal Positions & Affiliations

Berry, Francis, Seifman, Salamey & Harris
Senior Partner
50 years

American Bar Association

Michigan Bar Association

Detroit Bar Association

Cedars of Lebanon/Arab-American Bar Association
President
20+ years

Municipal Law Section
Michigan State Bar

National Institute of Municipal Law Officers

American Trial Lawyers Association

Michigan Supreme Court
Admitted to Practice
February 28, 1950

United States Supreme Court
Admitted to Practice
May 19, 1958

Business & Professional Posts

Dearborn Bank & Trust
Board of Directors, Member

Chrysler Dealership
Chairman
1956-1959

Berry Home Supply
Chairman
1958-1974

**Jimmy Carter's White House
Conference on Small Business**
Member
1980

The
Political
Arena

It is the duty of every citizen according to his best capacities to give validity to his convictions in political affairs.

Albert Einstein
German Theoretical Physicist
1879-1955

Chapter 8

16th Democratic Congressional District

Michael's venture into the political world began in 1948 with the first campaign of G. Mennen Williams, who was running for governor on the Democratic ticket against Victor E. Bucknell. Williams won the primary and proceeded to defeat the Republican incumbent. Williams would go on to win the governor's post seven times, which was unprecedented.

In the meantime Michael was active in the 16th Congressional District of the Democratic Party, which he joined in 1950. Not an avowed political zealot, he supported the Democratic nominees on the state and federal levels.

One of Michael's most cherished moments in the political spectrum came in 1960 when he served as the elector for the 16th District for the State of Michigan, casting all of district's votes for presidential candidate John Fitzgerald Kennedy.

[On a trip to Texas in 2006, Michael visited the Book Depository warehouse where Lee Harvey Oswald supposedly stood when he shot Kennedy. Although Michael did not entertain conspiracy theories that have surrounded Kennedy's assassination, he offered that Lyndon Johnson would have had the motivation.

"Because he inherited the post," Michael offers. "He was powerful without question in Texas and in the country, because much of the legislation that they attribute to Kennedy was never passed during his presidency, but after Johnson became president. Johnson had the power in both the Congress and the Senate.

"If you look at the human factor and observe other nations and how they progressed through assassinations, it's understandable, despite the fact that we think of ourselves as a moral country."]

Michael became a precinct delegate, then a member of the Executive Board and finally a member of the Democratic State Central Executive Committee, a position he retained until 1964. Michael accepted the nomination for chairmanship of the 16th District, opposing a man that claimed to have the backing of John Dingell, who was running for Congress for the first time in that district.

"It was interesting that the nominee, whether by accident or otherwise, was Polish, and John Dingell has Polish heritage. I think a great part of the party in the 16th District then was made up of Poles. I didn't have many sympathizers outside of labor at the time, but I remember a meeting down in River Rouge in which there was a somewhat heated discussion between my opponent's supporters and my group, labor. I stayed out of it naturally and so did the candidate of the opposition."

Michael prevailed, beating his opponent. "I think Dingell threw in his support. I'm not positive, but I had known Dingell from the practice of law. He had been an assistant prosecutor and a damned good one."

A meeting between labor and the Congressman took place after the election to show that no problem existed between the two factions. By the end of that meeting, there was unanimity. Under Michael's leadership from 1964 until he resigned in 1972, the 16th Congressional District became one of the two most powerful districts in the state of Michigan.

"We had a great deal of unity. We had the support. I was then a labor-oriented chairman of the district, and people on the outside would say, oh, he's controlled by labor. That wasn't true. Believe me, labor never asked me to do anything that was not in conformity with a sense of fairness and fair play."

"Mike was one of the best district chairmen I ever had," says Congressman Dingell. "He was smart as all get out and he had a great sense of policy and public interest. He's very sensitive. Mike's an honest man. He kept the district in good shape. I never had to worry about that. I've had a bunch of good chairmen; in fact, I've never had a chairman I didn't respect, admire, and love. That goes back 50 years. They're the people you rely on to protect your rear. Mike was amongst the best of them."

Frank Kelley well remembers the effectiveness of Michael Berry's leadership in the 16th District. "In my judgment, at that time, of all the chairpersons in Michigan – and there were probably as many as 25 of them – obviously Mike was the most effective. He was the most articulate and by party leadership he was the most respected chairperson. Point being, he was recognized early on as a very skilled politician in the best sense of that word and was respected by all the party leadership and elected officials."

To fill an attorney general vacancy, Frank Kelley had been appointed to that office. Nine months later, a virtual unknown, he had to run for office, campaigning all around the state.

"In all of the large congressional districts in Wayne and Oakland counties, Mike's 16th District always had the largest attendance, at least two or three to one over any other district," he recalls. "People came out. They came to his meetings. His delegates were active and politically sophisticated. He had a good organization, probably the best of any congressional district, and that impressed me. As a candidate facing election, it was comforting to know that in his district, there were all of these highly skilled troops who were going to be able to get out the vote of our party during the campaign and on Election Day."

In the capacity of 16th Congressional District Chairman, Michael Berry handled the endorsement of candidates and the elections. They developed an International Night each year in which they brought together members of the diverse communities in the district.

"They call for diversity in everything today. Well, we had it back then in the 50s, 60s, and 70s."

Strength in unity

"I think Mike's success was built on the fact that he did so much for Arabs," says Clarence Contratto, a political heavyweight in Dearborn. "Dearborn wouldn't be what it was then or is today without Mike Berry. He brought more people here from the old country and helped them get started. Mike and I sat down in the very, very beginning when Arabs were not welcomed in the Democratic Party. Everyone looked at them as odd balls, but Mike and I sat down with some of the key leaders at that time and said, 'The doors are open. Come on in.' We were the first to give them seats on State Central and committee assignments within the 16th District. Congressman Dingell, Mike, and I really pushed for that."

In the 1960s, the 16th Congressional District was the largest in the United States. "It stretched from West Grand Boulevard all the way to the Ypsilanti line, and from Delray in Downriver all the way north to Dearborn Heights," explains Clarence. "That was before we had one man/one vote, which we have now. There were 32 municipalities in our district.

"When we opened Democratic headquarters, we had a team. We were the first to design the unity slate, which was made up of Congressman Dingell, Mike Berry, Clarence Contratto for the UAW and Charlie Younglove for the Steelworkers. We all sat down together and pretty much made the decisions about who would get the nod and who wouldn't. If anybody in any of these 32 municipalities wanted to run for city council or mayor or judge, they went through us.

"Charlie and Mike clashed a lot, but Charlie was the kind of guy that when he sat down in a committee, he wanted to rule it, but we wouldn't let him. We were at that time bigger. This wasn't about one person; it was a foursome."

Homework

When Michael was chairman of the 16th Congressional District and Clarence Contratto was with him at the podium, they encountered conditions ripe for war on many occasions. "Some of the district conventions were so rough, we had to appoint several sergeants-at-arms – police from different cities that were good Democrats," recalls Clarence. "We would put the rabble-rousers in the basement at the Ukrainian Hall on Oakman Boulevard. We had to separate the crowd, because sometimes they would break out in fist fights.

"At the podium, I always used to say to Mike, 'My God, Mike, look at this. We're going to get our ass whipped today.' And Mike would always say, 'Naw, naw. Just relax. Look, you've done your homework; I've done mine. We've got the votes. When you've got the votes, kill 'em with kindness. Don't panic and don't get mad at them. Just sit here and watch and smile at them. As long as you've done your homework and have your people coming, we'll win.' And we did. We never lost.

"We always had a little caucus at Mike's office before each convention, and everyone was given an assignment. Mine was to make sure we had all the UAW people out. This was the way Mike operated. Mike didn't walk into a meeting and try to do something. He started weeks in advance."

Robert Kennedy

Michael Berry's walls at home are lined with letters from many U.S. Presidents, cabinet members, and other influential politicians. They have written to Michael to show their appreciation for his wise counsel over matters domestic and foreign.

ROBERT F. KENNEDY

May 20, 1968

Mr. Michael Berry
2015 Cadillac Towers
Detroit, Michigan

Dear Mike:

I sincerely appreciated the opportunity to meet
with you in Detroit.   It afforded me the chance
to establish a direct line of communication.   I
do hope in the campaign weeks ahead, we can again
discuss problems of mutual concern.

I am sure, both you and I agree, that the Middle
East situation should be, and must be, of grave
concern of the United States government.

Allow me again to express my sincere thanks for
coming to the airport and meeting at the hotel.

Sincerely,

Robert F. Kennedy

Robert Kennedy is one example. His letter refers to a ride that Michael gave him from the airport in Detroit and to their discussion about the Middle East. They dined at the Pontchartrain Hotel.

"The conversation centered on the failure of the United States to level the playing field in its treatment of the Arab World," explained Michael. "I thought the United States should have a more evenhanded approach to its foreign policy in the Middle East and not just turn over everything lock, stock, and barrel to the Israelis, which at that time took place and it still continues to this day."

Robert Kennedy was assassinated on June 6, 1968, not long after his visit with Michael. Kennedy's letter – dated May 20, 1968 – arrived a week or two later.

1968 Democratic Convention – Chicago

In 1968, as the National Democratic Convention was approaching, Michael needed to decide which delegates would go to the convention. In addition to the four that were to be elected delegates, the district created an alternate delegate category, giving them four additional representatives. It was a rather heated time.

Michael received a call from labor, because the slate of delegates and alternates he had prepared did not include state senators from the district – Roger Craig, a dear friend, and Eddie Robinson, a bright young man. "Labor asked me why we did not appoint these two state senators as delegates to the national convention," Michael recalls. "I pointed out that I felt they had not worked in the vineyards long enough to be entitled to delegate posts. However, I agreed with labor to give them the opportunity to be heard."

Soon afterwards, a meeting took place at Michael's home. In attendance, in addition to the two senators, were Rev. Willoughby, a Presbyterian minister who represented the liberal section of the Democratic Party in the 16th District, Iris Becker, a teacher for whom Dearborn's Becker School is named, and Clarence Contratto. Michael especially enjoyed Iris, a very fiery heavyset woman and a good speaker.

The long drawn-out session lasted into the wee hours of the morning. Vivian served various cheeses, olives, tea, coffee and some sweets, as they tried to hammer out the problem of delegates and alternates.

"I agreed to name one of them as an alternate delegate to the national convention. Eddie Robinson felt he had more power than that and he turned around and said to Roger Craig, 'Roger, do you think this district would condone our being delegated to alternate posts and not as full delegates? I'm willing to take my chances and prove that we have more power, if you will, than to be relegated to alternate positions, just one of us.'

"My response at that time was, 'Eddie, let me ask you, have you counted noses? Do you know what you're getting into?'"

"Yeah," he said, "I know, and I think Roger will agree with me that we're willing to take on the District on this one."

The district did make the decision. Michael left it up to them. That was around 2:30 a.m. They all parted on a friendly basis, but Michael knew what they were going to do. They put the machinery in motion.

"We created a slate, which gave us four delegates, four alternates, and a new one, an alternate's alternate, so that several people could go to Chicago. Was that historic? Yes."

The next day was the election at the 16th District convention, which made the meeting the night before all the more important. Michael called Doug Fraser, then vice president of the UAW, and explained that they offered the state senators an alternate spot on the slate, but they did not accept. As a result, the determination of who would go to Chicago was going to go to a vote on the convention floor at the district level.

"Needless to say, all of our delegates, our alternate delegates and the alternates' alternate were all from our slate. They didn't even get one position, but ultimately they got to Chicago on behalf of some other group that got them in. Maybe just because they were senators, they got to go."

Rioting started even before the delegates and alternates went to Chicago. Dearborn's Chief of Police was in the 16th District at the local convention, which was held at the Ukrainian Hall on Oakman Boulevard.

"It started with some members from my group getting involved with some members of Roger and Eddie's group," says Michael. "They engaged in a fist fight, and someone called the Dearborn police. A couple of guys were bloodied up, and the police took them to get first aid. No police report was ever filed on the incident. I think that was primarily because the chief was a member of our executive committee. That's just my belief. I don't know for a fact if he interceded or not, but I suspect that it did take place."

History surely has relegated the 1968 Democratic National Convention to the book of unforgettable convention memories. On the heels of the assassinations that year of Dr. Martin Luther King, Jr. and Robert Kennedy and widespread anti-war protests, the Democratic Party convened in Chicago to nominate its candidate for president.

"It was the hippies' invasion," recalls Michael. "They disrupted a lot of the meetings and the convention itself. While we were walking down the streets in Chicago, we saw a Mercedes stretch limousine being driven by a kid wearing a red bandana on his head. I was flabbergasted at seeing a car that at the time had to be worth at least $50,000; it was a costly piece of machinery, being driven by a hippy.

"That, in addition to what we read but did not see, included some of the hippies, who were living in many of the high-rise apartments and hotels. They were dropping bags of excrement onto the police officers below."

The clash between protesters and police on the streets of the Windy City echoed across the country and around the world as the media widely publicized the events. Hard-liner Mayor Richard J. Daley refused permits for rallies and marches and called for use of force, if necessary to quell the angry throngs, only to exacerbate the problem.

Police used Billy clubs and tear gas against news people and protesters, including some notables, like Hugh Hefner and Winston Churchill's grandson, who were caught in the fray. National debates ensued about how Chicago handled the situations surrounding the convention.

In response to criticism, Mayor Daley delivered one of the most famous malapropisms of that era: "The policeman is not there to create disorder; the policeman is there to preserve disorder."

Michael was chairman of the 16th District delegation. "We were committed to Humphrey, although I permitted others to come in and speak to our group. When the roll call came, I cast all of our votes for Hubert Humphrey."

When all was said and done, however, the events of the 1968 Democratic National Convention changed history, changed the shape of political and cultural life, and doomed the presidential candidacy of Hubert Humphrey.

In every serious set of events, one humorous one usually crops up, and the following is no exception. Michael tells it best.

"One evening, Thornton Hopson, Frank Nizio, Clarence Contratto, another person, and I got into a cab. I asked the driver to take us to Diamond Jim's, where I had enjoyed a wonderful steak on an earlier trip to Chicago. The driver acknowledged that he knew the place. However, instead of taking us to Diamond Jim's, he took us to Jim Diamond's. Apparently he received some kind of commission for fares that he dropped off there.

"We sat down and ordered steaks. The waiter asked if we wanted mushrooms, and we said, yes. That's when we discovered to our dismay that it was not the same restaurant where I had dined the previous year. When the waiter brought the steaks to our table, we were hypnotized by the fact that we could not see the steaks."

Frank took his fork and lifted one mushroom after another, demanding with his heavy Polish accent, "Where is the steak?"

"Under the mushrooms," the waiter replied.

When they got the bill, Thornton Hopson said, "Let me pay this one." So he paid it and received a few pennies in change. He put two cents on the table.

The waiter asked, "Where's my tip?"

Thornton replied, "Right there. That's all you're worth."

Political savvy

Whether Michael Berry was settling squabbles on the local political scene, drumming up support for a well-deserved candidate for public office or representing his congressional district at a national party convention, he was always thinking one or two moves in advance.

"I think he must have played chess in his day," says Russ Gibb. [Actually, the game was checkers, according to David Berry, one of Michael's second cousins. "Mike used to play checkers with my father, and my dad was the best. Everyone tried to beat him, but no one could."]

"He's always a move ahead," says Russ. "He knows where something is going. When you and I might get hung up with a situation for a moment, he'd say, 'Well, if this happens, that will happen.' He's a consequence person...a masterful politician.

"Mike's American. Yes, he's very proud of his ethnicity, but that's what makes him outstanding. He's American and then of Arab descent.

L to R: Michael Berry, U. S. Senator Phil Hart, and a senatorial aide

He's not a hyphenated Arab American.

"Does he have a tough side to him? Oh, yeah! He can get tough when he wants to get tough. Mike has been on the planet longer than I have, and he's a classic example of a man with an incredible amount of common sense and wisdom through experience."

"Michael Berry was driven by several things," notes Congressman John Dingell. "First of all, Michael is a good lawyer. Second, he's a good Democrat with a large "D" and a small "d". He also believes in doing good and helping people. He is proud of his Arab heritage and he tries to help his people. He is also, by instinct and by nature, a very hard-working man. He's got a very good heart and he tries to help people whenever he can.

"We never thought of Mike as an Arab or anything else. He was Michael Berry. Michael wasn't pigeon-holed or cataloged."

Local political clout

The late Wayne County Probate Judge George Bashara recalls the power, the clout that Michael Berry wielded in his political prime.

"He was at one time, I sincerely believe, one of the most powerful Democrats in the State of Michigan. He had a great influence on who became governor and who filled other seats in state government. He was particularly influential when it came to appointing judges.

"Mike was one of my earliest supporters in 1969 when I was appointed as a Wayne County Probate Judge by a Republican governor – William Milliken. Under our constitution, once you are appointed, you have to run in the next general election, which meant I had to run in 1970. The gentleman who was running against me was John Patrick O'Brien, who was very well known, the top vote-getter in the Common Pleas Court in Detroit. He went on to become the perennial vote-getter in the Recorder's Court for the City of Detroit until they became circuit judges.

"My father had been a particular foe of the hotel and restaurant workers union and, as a result, Judge O'Brien's supporters used whatever they could get hold of to show that. They considered my father to be anti-union, which he was not, but they tried to fasten that label on me.

"I don't know anyone that worked harder for my election than Mike Berry. He tried very hard to get me the UAW endorsement. The night before the UAW's Committee on Political Education was to meet to decide where their endorsement should go – and I had been given reasonable hope to think I would get it – O'Brien's supporters put on the chair of every delegate to the committee a newspaper article referring to my father as "Injunction Bashara", because he had secured an injunction against some very unfortunate and improper tactics on the part of union organizers in the hotel and restaurant workers union, which really had nothing to do with the UAW, but it was a union nonetheless through the AFL.

"Mike worked very hard even during that conference to get me the UAW endorsement. It didn't come out as he hoped, because of that newspaper article, but Mike did secure the endorsement of the 16th Congressional Democratic District, of which he was chairman.

"I won that election by 95,000 votes, and I sincerely believe that Mike Berry, as well as my mentor Judge Frank Szymanski of the Probate

Court, who was very strong in the Polish community, had about as much to do with my winning as anything. I've never forgotten it.

"I was a Republican and I have supported a lot of Republican candidates, but during that time, Mike forgot about politics, because he thought I was the most qualified person for the job and because he knew me.

"I have had a lot of successes in my life, and whenever I see Mike, I always give him credit for a lot of them. He's never asked me for anything. From time to time, he would call and ask if I knew somebody and would I do them a favor, but it has never been for anything for himself personally. He was very proud that I was on the bench and thought I was doing a good job."

Ethnic perspective

Michael Berry was an ethnic leader before ethnicity was in vogue. "He happened to be operating in a city that was run by Orville Hubbard, an extremely strong and disciplined administrator, who might have had conflicts with that ethnicity," recalls Frank Kelley.

"Not only was Mike from a fairly invisible minority in terms of the general population at that time, but he was Muslim as well. It was the measure of the man, because he was a true Muslim, a devoted Muslim, as much as he could be living in the world of politics.

"At the same time, he was a democratic type person and, as a result, many leaders of other religions – Jews, Christians, and others – have said to me what a wonderful person Michael Berry is and what a wonderful diplomat he is and how much they respect him. So, he did have that facility of accommodating himself and ingratiating himself with groups of other origins without having to sacrifice his own identity. People respected him and liked him. They still do."

Linda Bazzi applauds Michael Berry for not hiding his ethnicity or religion. "I can't imagine where Arab Americans would be today if Mike had taken the easy way out by disowning his nationality and religion. For that we thank him. Back in the 60s and 70s, a lot of people came from Lebanon, and they disowned their heritage. They changed their names and did things so they would not be associated with being a Muslim. My generation is very proud of Mike because he was honest, straightforward, and not afraid of anyone. He told it the way it was."

Local Arab-American politics

Michael has been a strong proponent of Chicago-style districting for Dearborn. "If the city were in districts, people could elect someone that really represents them, like the Arab Americans. They don't really have a chance. They're growing, but it's going to be a way down the road. I think in another 10 years, at their rate of growth, they will be a force to contend with.

"Some of our people take advantage of their ethnic background and work not for their ethnicity but for themselves, and this is something I've objected to and raised holy cane over in my community. And I still do it, every time I seen an inequity."

Although Michael Berry recommended the formation of an Arab American political action committee, he now strongly opposes it, for the very reasons just cited.

"The young man and his father sat in my living room, when I suggested that the first things they could do to help the Arab American community would be to form a PAC and become active in politics. The young man did that and later came back and requested $300, which later became the established rate for membership. I gave it to him. I attended two meetings, but I immediately saw that it was a self-serving and self-promoting organization. So I wrote a letter resigning and sent a copy to the *Arab American News*.

"Osama Siblani [publisher of the *Arab American News*] and I get along fine, but what he says he's going to do, he either forgets or neglects to do them. He talks to me and tells me all these things he intends to do and then fails to perform. Many, many years ago when he and his wife started the newspaper, they interviewed me. Osama has good command of the language, and he's a good thinker on his feet. He has done very well on television when he debates people on issues, and I like his style. Osama is now president of AAPAC."

Provincialism and tribalism

A few years ago, someone accused Michael of being one-sided in that he was fighting for the Lebanese, and that he told the Wayne County Executive that the person he hired did not represent the Arabic community, but just a segment of Palestinians.

"That's not true," Michael says, "because when my accuser – a Palestinian attorney in Dearborn – accused me of being one-sided, I told him, 'Long before you were born, I was here making a pitch for the Palestinians. When we had hardly any kind of an Arab community, I was fighting the cause.'"

"Mike has always been against tribalism or provincialism," notes Tallal Turfe. "A lot of people come from south Lebanon, and they bring their villages with them and create tribalism here. A number of these village tribes have their own social clubs. Mike believes that when they are in America, they should understand that they are in a new atmosphere and a new environment, so it does not bode well for prejudice.

"Mike thought people should intermingle with other tribes or provincial villages and intermarry, even with other cultural groups, not always Arab marrying Arab. It is good for the blood to circulate for the genes and heredity, but this concept is very difficult, especially with immigrants who have just arrived in America. They are undereducated, because of the long years of war in Lebanon."

"You can't win," says Michael. "It's a problem that we have. It's in our genes to never unite. There's a great deal to say if you can get people in a village to unite. It's a big thing, just in the village. Provincialism is part of our heritage, and tribalism is, too. That's something I've concluded we have to live with. It's our culture."

Another position Michael has held fast to is that of dual languages in education. "He was always against the grain on that issue," recalls Barry Seifman. "That's not the common ground in Dearborn. The reason why he took that position was 'Hey, we're Americans. We should know the language.' It's not that people shouldn't know their other language; it should not be their principle language here in America. It's the same for people who bring their village life here and think they can live as they did in the old country. They're not part of the community around them; they isolate themselves."

Chapter 9

Wayne County Road Commission

With the growth of the automobile industry came the Wayne County Parks System, founded by Edward Hines and other local leaders that pioneered for good roads at the turn of the century. Hines campaigned for the passage of the County Road Law in 1893, and he became one of the first Wayne County Road Commissioners, along with John Haggerty and William Butler.

Belle Isle Park, Hines Park, and others fell under the jurisdiction of the Road Commission. Lack of funding eventually brought the demise of park development in Wayne County, and other political problems beset the Road Commission.

In 1967, Alex Barber was a member of the Road Commission. He wielded a lot of power in the county. When he died on the way back from the Hawaiian Islands, the UAW nominated Michael Berry. "Because Barber was a labor man with the AFL, the UAW wanted me to take his place."

Before the election, one of the important players was Jerry Cavanagh, mayor of the City of Detroit. He sent Joseph B. Sullivan, who became a judge on the circuit bench, to talk to Thornton Hopson and insisted that Michael come from Florida to meet with him.

"Thornton picked me up at the airport and we met Joe in a downtown bar," Michael recalls. "He said he thought it would be a wise thing for me to withdraw, because he said they wanted Alex, my opponent from Taylor Township. I said, 'No, I can't do that. I've already committed.' The next day, I got word that Mayor Cavanagh was supporting me. He threw his 25 delegates in my corner and that was the deciding factor that motivated others to follow suit. I won the post decisively, beating my opponent decisively, many thanks to the UAW."

Mike Zolik, a civil engineer, who worked for the Road Commission for 33 years, well remembers Michael's arrival on the commission. "We knew he was a lawyer. We knew that he came with a reputation of being a tough man. Michael was not one to make decisions quickly. He wanted to know the lay of the land, and he wanted to learn about the people who he would be dealing with – me, the head of the legal department, the head of the engineering department, and Jim Davey, the managing director. Mike Berry respected Jim a great deal."

"He (referring to Jim Davey) made my life easier at the Road Commission," says Mike. "He was there as an advisor. He knew more about county government than any man I knew then or have known since. Jim was without question probably the best administrator I have ever met."

Bette Misuraca, who worked for Jim Davey, immediately recognized Michael Berry as all business. "When they brought Mike around and introduced him, he seemed a little – I don't want to say pompous – but he certainly seemed proud and reserved. He didn't really seem approachable. He was strictly business. But over the years, I found that Mike has a big heart."

Michael also established boundaries that he would not cross. On one occasion, Bette asked Michael to help a friend's son get a labor job for the summer. Michael asked to see his application, and he followed through.

Since Bette thought the boy would not thank Michael for the job, she decided to show her appreciation for granting the favor she requested. "I noticed that he always wore large beautiful ties, so I took a tie to his office along with an old portrait painting in an old frame that someone had thrown out of an antique shop. It was a painting of a horse in full gait, running. I thought Mike would love it for his office."

When Bette presented the gifts to Michael, he thanked her but said he would keep only the portrait. He returned the tie to her.

"Don't you like the tie?" Bette asked.

"The picture has no monetary value," Michael replied, "but to me it is great, because I love horses and I love the portrait."

Bette felt mixed emotions. No one in the office had ever turned down a "Bette tie"; in fact, everyone had one from her.

"I've thought it over as time has passed. He did not keep the tie because it was the ethical thing to do."

Decision-making

"When items came before the board for consideration, the determination of whether or not they would be approved, Mike was especially curious," Mike Zolik relates. "He wanted to recognize the professionalism of each person in his particular field, because each was well versed. He also wanted to know that they did everything that should be done in reaching their decisions to recommend an item to the board.

"So, in that way, Mike was a tough taskmaster. First, you had to be able to anticipate his questions, and then you had to be prepared to answer them. Most of the time, those of us who sat around the table at the commission meetings on Thursdays soon began to learn that there was not going to be any sloppy work there. And there wasn't. We all made mistakes.

"Once, I did something I should not have done or if I had explored something I would not have done it, and Mike said to me, 'I may chastise you for making a mistake, but I would be more critical of you if you didn't do something.' He didn't like inaction. He didn't want someone coming to the board and saying, well, here is the problem, here are the options, you decide.

"That was not Mike's style. Whether or not he agreed with you, he wanted you to tell the board members if an item should be approved or not. We had to make sure we considered every possibility. He knew something about chemistry, so he was particularly tough on the lab, where we had an engineer. In answering a question, Mike did not simply accept a yes or no; he wanted to know why you said yes or no."

Two cases, one involving fertilizer used in Wayne County Parks, and the other, road and signage paint quickly established Michael Berry as a commissioner who would not let issues pass lightly. His toughness became apparent in situations where work was sloppy or decisions were reached without adequate research and consideration of the facts.

Fertilizer bids

In the first few weeks that Michael was on the board, the commission wanted to confirm a purchase order for fertilizer of several tons. Michael saw that there was only one bid and asked the reason for one bid. He was told that only one manufacturer made KCLO-4, a substance that the chemist for the Road Commission mixed with water and used to fertilize fairways, lawns and parks in Wayne County.

"I frankly don't know how many tons or bags were purchased, but it was not a small item," Michael says. "Then it hit me. From my background in chemistry, I knew that KCLO-4 was a very unstable substance in that if it were mixed with water the one atom of oxygen would break up and go out into the air. That would leave KCLO-3 actually as the remaining substance, which would mix with the water and provide the nutrients that were needed."

The chemist said Michael was wrong. Michael offered one way to determine who was right. They could test it.

"I asked if there were other companies that manufactured KCLO-3, as that was all they needed. And, yes, there were a number of such companies, but they said that KCLO-4 was a far better nutrient. The staff at the Road Commission, especially the chemist, made that assertion.

"So like a stupid idiot, I issued a challenge to the chemist, and I suggested that we hire an independent lab. I thought that was a very simple thing. We could get the Detroit Testing Lab to give us this information. All we had to do was to give a sample of each substance and tell Detroit Testing Lab to give us the breakdown.

"After three or four weeks, I kept bugging the staff, asking for the results. Well, apparently I had touched a nerve someplace. I was told that the stuff had not been submitted and Detroit Testing Lab had not been asked, and I said, well, okay, I'll pay for it. I'm going to call Detroit Testing Lab and tell them.

"Well, at our next regular meeting day – on the 7th floor of the City County building – when I walked in, I was asked to go into the back room. I did, with the other two commissioners, who at this point in time were neutral in their stance, because they had worked so many years with the staff and I was a newcomer. I was not the chairman at this point.

"The chemist for the Commission told me that I was correct, that my understanding of the breakup of KCLO-4 to KCLO-3 plus oxygen was the net result and that the residual KCLO-3 would have served just as well. I didn't want to make an issue out of it thereafter. I felt being new that I shouldn't create the kind of waves that would bring the press into this particular arena.

"So we set up new specs and secured a number of bidders. As a result, we realized great savings to Wayne County and to other counties across the state.

Road and Signage Paint bids

Another question arose shortly after bids were submitted for reflecting road and signage paint. At that time, Michael again noticed only one company had submitted a bid. When he inquired why, again he was told that there was only one manufacturer of this kind of paint, and the commission had to accept it. It was universal all over the country. Every state in the union bought from this company.

"I felt that was not a satisfactory answer," Michael said. "There must be other places that manufactured it. We should at least get an idea of the costs. I suggested they call the other countries – Germany and Japan – and look into it what they would charge us for the same product."

Michael personally called the German commercial attaché and asked him to send some information to the staff on the costs. "I was advised later that the paint – if my memory serves me correctly – was about $1/gallon less delivered to the docks here in Detroit, plus they would give us $3 back for the container, a 55-gallon drum. With our road system in Wayne County, that was a lot of roads to cover and a lot of signage."

They relayed this information to 3M and as a result 3M became extremely competitive and the Road Commission continued purchasing from them. But the net result was that not only Wayne County but also every county in the state of Michigan benefited from this bidding approach.

"When dealing with Mike Berry week after week after week, we found that he had great knowledge of a lot of things, maybe not tremendous knowledge, but in areas – like chemistry – that we would not have expected him to have," says Zolik. "That's why you had to be sure you covered all your bases before you went to him. You could not skip a base, because he would pick up on it."

Chairmanship

In Michael's second year on the Wayne County Road Commission, he became chairman. He remained in that position until he retired almost sixteen years later.

"Mike was especially tough when he was chairman," Zolik says. "If we wanted his approval, we had to have all our bases covered first. The other two board members, Mr. Krieger and for a while Mr. Neudack, were also tough to deal with, but Mike as chairman was especially tough."

As chairman, Michael Berry was most successful in the expansion work of Detroit Metropolitan Airport. "Other than that enormous responsibility and major contributions to the county and to the state, the basic thing that the Wayne County Road Commission did was to improve the infrastructure of Wayne County," notes Michael Guido, Mayor of Dearborn.

"They built roads, bridges, side-

Michael Berry, 1970s

walks, and public works projects in the heyday of cities when they had gravel roads. Mike helped transform Wayne County into this economic powerhouse where it was huge for industry as the arsenal of democracy. Ford, GM, Chrysler – they were all located in Detroit, Dearborn, Livonia, and Downriver, the steel mills by Zug Island – all of this industry. The Road Commission channeled the wealth of that industry into public improvements throughout the county. Mike spearheaded that effort."

"The Road Commission was the biggest thing in Wayne County," Congressman Dingell explains, "in terms of size, budget, money, and responsibilities. Mike was very active in putting the airport together. It was a big achievement. He laid the foundation."

Bette Misuraca agrees. "Mike had a very strong, urgent, and passionate plea about developing Metro Airport. Those who came after him would not have had anything to work with."

The engineering staff that the Road Commission had was a top-flight group. They foresaw the needs and they developed solutions as those needs became apparent to them. They already had in process the designs, plans, and specs for what they are doing now. "I understand that they claim they cast away those plans and are now putting in their own plans," Michael Berry suggests, "but if you could get your hands on the plans that Metro Airport had designed by the Road Commission staff, the plans and specs being utilized today were set up by the old staff.

"I don't know if it's politics or what, but I can tell you this, the staff of the Wayne County Road Commission was a superb group of engineers, administrators, and legal experts. They were a self-contained outfit that did a job, and that's why many other departments despised the Wayne County Road Commission...they considered we had too much power and were able to do things without having to report to any particular body. That may be true to a large degree but they had control of the Road Commission by way of electing the county commissioners, so the election and naming of commissioners was really in the hands of the county commission. That body was political in nature, but the staff was a highly competent group of men and women."

Michael Berry helped develop a great airport, but in the process he developed lives. He was about helping people and changing their lives. He did that by putting qualified people in jobs that gave them a better opportunity to grow and support their families.

Herschel Hogan started out as a laborer for the county. "That's the only way you could get into the county," explains Bette Misuraca. "You had to be a laborer, not start at the top like they do now. Herschel made about $6,000 a year, if that. He was such a humble man.

"He used to take care of Mike's cars. Now, he didn't work for Mike, but he worked in a public garage where Mike parked his cars, and when he wasn't busy, he would shine them for Mike, and I'm sure Mike would tip him. Herschel liked Mike, so he continued to take care of his cars.

"When Wayne County bought the Neudack Building at 415 Clifford (it was named after Phil Neudack, who preceded Mike on the Road Commission), they needed someone to work in the parking lot, take care of the cars, and make sure that the county cars were secure and didn't go in and out.

"Mike brought Herschel over there, and he started out as a laborer in that county owned parking lot, much cheaper than it could have been outsourced to do. It was the first real job with benefits that Herschel had. He had a wife and three or four children, so that was something.

"Through his dedication and ability, Herschel became the building manager of the Neudack Building before he died. He was in charge of all the boilers, the building, and maintenance. He knew how to do it, but he just never had been given that opportunity, so it gave him and his family a certain status that they never would have achieved without Mike's influence.

"Now, Herschel's two children have worked for the county – one in airport operations and the other, as an attorney. There must be millions of stories like this out there. Mike changed the destiny of that family and many, many others."

Another thing about Michael, with his worldwide connections, notes Grace Hampton, he could have gone to Washington and become a very wealthy attorney in an exclusive office somewhere, but he chose to be liberal and help black Americans and minority Arab Americans. "Having come up through Ford and with the UAW, he understood their plight and how they were left out of mainstream America. I believe it was his destiny to be that soldier…that advocate for the liberal cause. He waved the flag for justice and opportunity for all the people less fortunate than he was."

Michael gave Arab Americans the first opportunity to do well, but he stood on strong principles in the process. "We wanted him to be proud of us," said Linda Bazzi. "If someone came to him for a labor job, Mike would interview him. If the first question that person asked was, 'When can I get sick time, vacation time, or when can I go on disability?' that person never got the job. That was Mike."

Some of the appointments that he made then have proved their worth. They would not have had a chance to be in the system. "They have proven their worth," says Bette Misuraca, "so by Mike giving them that little window of opportunity for labor positions, they were able to contribute to the community and to their families, and to Mike's trust in them. Time has shown that Mike made the right decisions at that time."

Integration

Irma Clark-Coleman's first impression of Michael Berry was that he was the coolest guy. "I was just an administrative secretary; he was a commissioner. I worked on the [7th] floor, where the Board held its meetings, so I would see Mike come in. He always dressed real sharp and had beautiful cars. At one point, in 1975, he had a two-seater Mercedes, a gorgeous little Mercedes, which he parked in the public lot next door. When I would go out to lunch, I would see this beautiful car and I always said to myself, when I grow up, I want to be just like Mike Berry. He epitomized class and success in the right way. He was always friendly; success didn't spoil him. He spoke with everyone. He was a good judge of people, too.

"Mike was a tough chairman, and people really respected him, because he had heart. That's the only way I can describe it; he had compassion for other ethnicities. That may be because he's an American of Arab descent, and maybe he had suffered some discrimination. He knew what it felt like, so when he came into a position to help others, he did that.

"He integrated the Wayne County Road Commission. Before Mike came to the commission, it was chauvinistic, a man's world. They were more chauvinistic than they were against people of color. Women were like the bottom of the barrel. When Mike came aboard, there were no Arab Americans working at the Road Commission and very few black people.

"Before he was finished, he had transformed the Road Commission to reflect its location, the community it served. He made sure that a great number of blacks and Arab Americans were hired. Before that, the only positions that blacks or women had were entry level positions; blacks usually just did road repairs." Irma became one of the first black people to work for the Wayne County Road Commission.

"Because Mike integrated the Road Commission, he was soundly criticized. He drew a lot of heat for that, but he stood up to it. Mike Berry doesn't cave in to anything. He did the right thing, and when you do the right thing, you don't have reason to cave in to criticism."

Michael Berry International Terminal, 1974

Michael Berry International Terminal

No argument can be made that the Wayne County Road Commission, under the expert chairmanship of Michael Berry, succeeded in giving Michigan a world class airport. The aggressive expansion program included making substantial improvements and building parking decks. It was no surprise, then, that when the new international terminal was built, it would bear his name.

The dedication ceremonies took place on July 12, 1974. In the program for the event, the Board of the Wayne County Road Commission noted its achievements relative to the international terminal.

"The addition of this modern International Terminal will provide improved service with the major capitals of the world for all of Southeastern Michigan's aircraft and travelers. Other new facilities included in the expansion program are a 10,000-foot runway, improved lighting and taxiways on the airfield, expansion of the existing north and south terminals, a new auto parking deck, and new road systems into the airport, which are currently in the planning stages."

Jim Davey, Managing Director of the Road Commission, served as moderator for the dedication ceremonies. The keynote speaker was Edwin Newman, NBC news anchor and host of the "Today" show at that time.

"It was an exciting day for me," says Michael. "We had a band that provided festive music, and many dignitaries from all over the state and

L to R: Roman Gribbs, Detroit Mayor (1970-74), Michael Berry, Jerome P. Cavanaugh, Detroit Mayor (1962-70)

some from Washington, D. C. were on hand for the occasion."

Bette Misuraca helped plan the event. "It was an in-house event, but then no one heard Edwin Newman, because a Jamaican band was making so much noise, they drowned out his remarks.

"The next day, something happened to the building, and they were afraid it was going to collapse. They had to make sure the permits were in order. So, while we were dancing the Marenge, the walls could have caved in on the Michael Berry International Terminal. I think he never knew that...

"I kid Mike, 'You'd better stay alive, because when you die, they're going to take your name off that mid-field terminal.' We laugh about that. 'You'd better put it on some sort of granite so it can't be removed.'"

The dedication festivities were well attended by dignitaries and other notables, and by Michael's family, including his mother, Mariam.

Subsequent to the dedication of the Michael Berry International Terminal, Michael encountered some problems with Tom O'Rourke,

L to R: Jim Davey, Michael Berry, Edwin Newman

one of the commissioners. "He wanted Jim Davey's job when Jim retired, and we accommodated him in that regard. We thought he would settle down once he got a job that paid him $60,000 a year, which was the most money he had ever made.

Shortly thereafter, several arguments and conflicts arose between Tom and Michael. Tom wanted to control the board and to make decisions, which were the province of the board of the Road Commission. Michael refused to cave in to his requests and made it clear at a board meeting.

"The next day, after the board meeting, I was on my way back down to Florida, and Tom followed me there, but I did not know that. At 7 a.m., he called and asked if we could meet at the iHop nearby. I agreed and said I could be at the restaurant in 10 minutes. He said, 'I'm already waiting.'

Michael went to the restaurant, thinking it had to be something serious for Tom to follow him to Florida. When Michael arrived, he said, "I guess the county picks up the tab for your trip. Not mine, I paid my own

Michael Berry with his daughters (L to R): Carol, Gail, Cindi and Laura, 1974

way." This was one of the things Michael felt about being independent and not relying on any financial backing from the county.

One word led to another, and Tom finally said, "Either you resign or I quit."

"Tom, I don't think it's in your best interests to quit," Michael countered. "It's a job and a well paying job. I thought you were looking for this position for a long time, and now you want to quit.'

"Well, you and I are never going to get along, and it's going to be either you resign or I quit."

"There's no reason for me to resign," Michael said. "If you want to quit, go ahead and quit."

So he did. He resigned. Then Michael heard from various sources that Tom went to the FBI and what he said or did, Michael will never know.

"Some years later, the county executive told me that Tom had gone to the FBI and told them I was wielding so much power and there had to be something wrong, something nefarious, that I was doing. Apparently

Michael Berry & family, 1974

the FBI saw through him and started to investigate him. That's according to Ed McNamara, who was county executive then.

"Ed and I went way back to 1957, when I had a Chrysler and Plymouth dealership in Livonia in partnership with Sam Zehra, a dear friend, and Ed was a member of the city council there. I had represented him when he was a member of a subdivision and a school board member, and a builder was violating building restrictions. I took up their cause and we won. That's how I got to know Ed.

"When I was chairman of the Wayne County Road Commission, Ed was mayor of Livonia. He wanted certain things done, which we accommodated to the best of our ability. Our efforts maybe did not suit him at the time, but he finally accepted them."

When Ed McNamara was Wayne County Executive, he hired a lot of people. "He did things that I think were not exactly kosher," says Michael, "at least in my opinion. A couple of contracts were suspicious, based on newspaper reports. One involved a man who claimed he graduated from West Point, and he was on the front page of the papers. His son was hired by a company, and the owner of that company was a member of the Amicus Group here in Dearborn. An Italian immigrant, a

Mariam Berry, 1974

pretty sharp cookie, got the contracts from the county. One contract was allegedly valued at $850,000 – without a bid.

"When I was chairman of the Road Commission, anything over $500 had to be bid out. But this man's contract was not bid, according to the press. Subsequent to that, the $850,000 contract escalated into several million dollars, also without a bid, again according to the press. The son of the man, who is in charge of that division of the airport, along with his supervisor, released those contracts.

"Another contract was one in which McNamara awarded a million-dollar contract to a relative allegedly without bid, according to the press.

"So there were a series of things. They said the FBI was investigating further. Then Ed retired and it was announced that he had cancer. He died shortly thereafter.

The *Detroit News* attack

Beginning the end of April and running into May 1981, the *Detroit News* ran front-page articles on four consecutive days, as well as two editorials and some political cartoons. The focus of the series was on Michael Berry's role on the Wayne County Road Commission.

Joel Smith, an investigative reporter for the *Detroit News* came in and started investigating the Road Commission. "I had won two elections, two six-year terms," Michael recalls. "This guy had

Michael Berry, late 1970s

a hard-on without question. He was supposed to go after the Road Commission, but he singled me out because of my ethnicity. That was back in the time when we didn't believe in diversity. The *Detroit News* did not, at least not this reporter. I had hired a lot of blacks, Irish, everyone that really applied for a job, including Arab Americans. That was too much for him. That started the ball rolling in that direction.

"He cast a shadow over my career, saying that the Road Commission had purchased a screw for $11. That was true in a sense, only the decimal point had been placed behind the 11 instead of in front of it. It was an 11-cent screw. So this was the big deal.

"Then he thought he found that there was $250,000 worth of plywood missing. I don't know where he got his information, but probably from someone on the staff who didn't like the way I was handling things. Smith went on a rampage, but within two hours, we found the $250,000 worth of paneling. We called him in and pointed to where it was all stacked up. But he had already written the article; he never wrote that we found the plywood or that the screw cost 11 cents. In all his articles, he never wrote that I saved hundreds of thousands of dollars within the first three weeks of my appointment to the Road Commission."

"Mike was very strict, extremely strict," Dr. Avery Jackson reports. "When it came to penny for penny, he was to the penny. He didn't go by the round-off dollars. He didn't care for round-offs. If it ended up so many dollars and so many cents, it had to be in writing exactly like that. He was very tight on himself and on others in that regard particularly."

The media don't care, Michael asserts. "It's not their money. You see, I was brought up to understand that it's an honor to serve the people in a governmental capacity. I thought this was my purpose – to save money. The general public doesn't care how much you save. The newspapers don't care. They never bought up anything of the nature of good that I accomplished while serving on the Board. Every two years they used to change chairmanship, but after I became chairman, they didn't.

"When the *Detroit News* put me on the front page four days in a row, I used to read what they wrote, just to see what they would use to smear me. Frankly, I valued my reputation and thought I had done so much good. We saved the county money on insurance, too, and my county road commissioners were strict on maintaining the integrity of the bid process."

Michael received a call from another reporter suggesting that they meet. They met at the Sheik Café downtown. "Before I left the Road Commission office," Michael tells, "I took a sheet of paper and on the top, I put the words **Wayne County Road Commission Expense Account**. I put the paper in my inside pocket. I figured the first thing we were going to discuss was expense accounts."

During the conversation over lunch, the reporter said, "Let me ask you, how much of the county's money did you spend during your years of service with the county?"

Michael said, "Do you mean this year?"

She said, "No, could you give me an idea – a ballpark figure – for the total number of years you've served up to now, how much have you spent?"

Michael had anticipated this, so he pulled out the sheet of blank paper.

"There is nothing on it," the reporter said.

"That is exactly right," Michael retorted.

Michael's salary for road commissioner was $8,000 for the first four years and $10,000 for the remaining 12 years. It was supposed to be a part-time job. "By the time I retired, the Road Commission was taking over 60 percent of my time. My main thought when I went in was to treat and spend the county's money like it was my own from the standpoint of being a good steward."

Bette Misuraca believes that the personalities of Joel Smith and Michael Berry clashed and that was one reason Joel took on Michael. "Mike would not cow-tow to Joel. Mike was not a politician; he was a king-maker. He worked behind the scenes making great politicians and always supported them through votes, financial contributions, and so on. I think he was not careless with what he said.

"Also, I think the folks from Grosse Pointe were very much afraid of the Arab and Muslim influence on the county, and they had to negate that by attacking. Had Mike not been in the position he was in, the Road Commission might have lasted a lot longer, so it was an attack on his nationality and his religion."

Jim Davey related to Michael that The *Detroit News* wanted to eliminate the Road Commission. "That desire went all the way back to the 50s," says Michael, "and that stemmed, I was told so it's hearsay, from the fact that the Wayne County Airport was established at its present site and not in Oakland County where the *Detroit News* wanted it. As a net result, there was a continuous ill feeling. The press was never kind to the Wayne County Road Commission. When I say press, I mean basically the *Detroit News*.

"Thereafter, this disharmony prevailed; any little upsurge in price of food at the airport would come down in a front page article on how bad the airport was managed.

"We had the plans for this development," Michael explains, referring to the mid-field terminal. "They may have just taken those and made some changes, but this mid-field terminal – the extensions – was all a product of the staff of the Wayne County Road Commission when I was chairman. I believe Mike Zolik will bear me out on this."

The *Detroit News* also charged Michael with nepotism, yet in his 15 years on the Road Commission, he appointed only 44 Arab Americans to county positions (labor jobs). That is an incredibly low number to use as the basis of an accusation, when the total number of employees exceeded 2000 when Michael became a member of the Road Commission.

"During my tenure as Road Commissioner Chairman for the longest period of time of any person in that capacity since its inception," Michael explains, "I hired a number of Arab Americans, because I felt they had not been given the opportunity to work."

One of the job placements that fueled the nepotism charge was Tim Ward, the husband of Carol, Michael's second daughter. When Tim graduated from Western Michigan University, Michael hired him into the sewage treatment plant as a laborer. "That's the only place that needed an employee," Michael says, "I told him, 'You take the tests and improve your status.'

"Tim took the Civil Service tests and moved up the ladder over a period of years. When the time and opportunity came for him to run for the managing director's job at the airport, he took the test. There were no shortcuts, no special favors because he was my son-in-law."

Joel Smith asked Michael if he was going to quit. "I said I would not quit while this cloud was hanging over my head. He used that in one of his articles, but he twisted it in a way to say there was a cloud over my head as far as my dealings were concerned. The only thing they had was that I hired Arab Americans, but I honestly feel now that the problem was not my management style but that I had hired a number of Arab Americans into the road system. Well, all of our hires were qualified."

"Michael Berry was a good commissioner, a completely honest one," Congressman Dingell asserts. "He took a lot of lumps, and I think they were entirely unjust. The media in these kinds of situations never admit they are wrong. He had some good articles afterwards which kind of said they were sorry but not that they were sorry for having said thus and so. That's the way the media is. Michael ran a clean, honest shop. The Road Commission was the biggest thing in Wayne County, in terms of size, budget, money, and responsibilities. Michael loved public service. He never profited from it, nor did he seek to. He just was out to do good, and it pleased him to do good. It still does."

Only one member of the Arab American community came to Michael's defense after the Detroit News attack. In the only letter to the editor published by that newspaper came from 17-year-old Sandra Amen (now Sandra Amen Bryan). "I simply wanted to say that I felt the charges against Michael Berry were so unfair. He was an honest man, who set out to do the right thing and help a lot of people in the process. None of the criticism expressed by the *Detroit News* was founded on reality. It was just so unfair."

Charles Farmer, the circuit court judge who had administered the oath to Michael Berry when he was appointed to the Road Commission, keenly observed Michael's performance all the years he served in that capacity. "In my opinion, Mike Berry lived up to the letter of that oath."

Double-crossed

When an organization or county department becomes very powerful, someone is bound to come along and try to clip its wings. The Wayne County Road Commission and the Drain Commission were supposed to be just county departments, but they became autonomous with their own boards that ran them.

"The late Freddie Burton, Sr. was managing director of the Road Commission in 1982, when Bill Lucas – then a Democrat – ran for Wayne County Executive," recalls Irma. "Freddie convinced the other commissioners to support Bill. On their own time, they worked hard, raised a lot of money, and provided a lot of volunteers. Bill Lucas got human and financial resources through the Road Commission. We campaigned for him, including Mike Berry.

"The first thing Bill Lucas did after he got elected was to eliminate the Road Commission! In March 1983, he had his staff collect petitions to put it on the ballot to get rid of Mike Berry and the Road Commission, Charlie Youngblood and the Drain Commission, and several other commissions. I don't think Freddie ever got over that. He had worked so hard to get Bill Lucas elected; he couldn't believe Bill would double-cross him and those who helped him get elected. Freddie died three months later. They said it was cancer, but it was aggravated by the disillusionment.

"See, Bill had no control over the Road Commission, which was one of his departments, so he had to get rid of it. He was backed by Oakland County Republicans, which we obviously hadn't known at the time. They convinced him that in order for him to have total control as Wayne County Executive, he had to get rid of everyone not under his control. That's what he did.

"When the Board was eliminated, that's when Mike Berry left. He was hurt, because he was not used to people double-crossing him like Bill Lucas did."

Freddie Burton, Sr. and Michael Berry, Retirement party, May 27, 1982

Keeping in touch

Since the days when they worked on the Road Commission, Michael Berry and Irma Clark-Coleman have kept in touch, along with Bette Misuraca and others.

With Michael, it was always about doing for people of other ethnicities, not just Arab Americans. As an American first, he believes in helping his fellow Americans, regardless their ethnic background.

After working for Wayne County for 31 years and serving as president of the school board for three years, Irma, a trail-blazer who opened many doors for fellow black women, was approached by Maxine Berman, who was looking for women to run for the Michigan Legislature. She convinced Irma to run for the House.

"I talked to Mike," Irma says. "He gave me some good tips on who to seek endorsements from and how to go about that. Then when the Michigan senate seat became available, I had even more reason to talk to Mike. The lines had been redrawn, and the new senate seat included 40 percent of Dearborn. Of course, Mike Berry is the Grand Poo-bah in Dearborn, so he was the first person I called. He said, 'Sure, let's have lunch.'

"By the time I arrived, Mike had assembled a group of the movers and shakers in Dearborn. He just walked me through that whole Dearborn portion of the campaign. The important part is when Mike Berry speaks, people listen. When Mike Berry said, 'This is my choice', that just parted the waters. From that point on, everything else fell in line. I won that senate seat, and just won re-election in November 2006.

"Throughout my whole career, Mike Berry has been the one stable force that I could always go to for good, sound advice, and he never wanted anything in return. He never asked me to do him a favor. He just took satisfaction out of being able to help. That's why I always call him my mentor, because he has such depth of knowledge. You can ask him about anything, and he will know about it. Even at his age now [86], he's still a mover and shaker. Everywhere I go, I still see him."

The
Family

Try to live your life so you wouldn't be afraid to sell the family parrot to the town gossip.

Will Rogers
American Author & Political Commentator
1879-1935

Introduction

We have seen Michael Berry overcome the struggles of poverty during the Great Depression and its aftermath. We have witnessed his success as an accomplished attorney, powerful politician, and highly effective chairman of the Wayne County Road Commission.

Now we look at a more personal side. After his father died in 1964, Michael assumed the role of head of the family, the patriarch, even though he was not the eldest in the family, Patricia says. "He took care of us. He was extremely good to my parents and to my mother and me. Whenever he and his family went on vacation, the majority of the time, he would take Mother and me with them.

"Our parents always said Mike came by leadership naturally. He was a born leader, and that was true in the family, in the community, in his work, in political activities, and whatever else he did.

"He loves people and he loves helping them. He loves the action. I think that's what keeps him going. It's good for him and it keeps him young."

Michael has given his heart and soul to raising wonderful, responsible, loving children. After the tragic loss of Michael and Vivian Berry's first born, the young couple looked forward with great anticipation to having more children.

They both had come from families with strong parents, full of life and love, who taught their children the values that transcend time – faith, love, learning, work, and a great sense of humor. Indeed, parenting is a skillful balance of love and discipline, work, and play. Parents must know when to hold on and when to let go, when to lay down the law and when to let laughter rule.

Michael and Vivian soon grew a fine family of four daughters, in order: Laura, Carol, Gail, and Cindi. Although Michael was a strict, protective father, perhaps borne out of the loss of his first son, he nurtured them and nourished them. He instilled in them the same values his parents had given him. He made sure they were well fed and cared for.

Back row (L-R): Cindi & Ray LaCroix, Tim & Carol Ward; Front row: Cindy Hanes & Michael Berry

He taught them right from wrong and respect for others regardless of ancestry or faith. He took great strides in assuring that each daughter felt appreciated for her uniqueness and her individuality, regardless where that led her.

Most of the people who contributed stories and memories to this book remarked about his love of family, his devotion to giving them the best that life can offer, and his steadfast support of their endeavors.

Each of the next four chapters is given to the four girls – in order of their birth – Laura, Carol, Gail, and Cindi. The fifth chapter deals with the great family tragedy of Vivian's untimely death, and the remaining chapters reveal how Michael moved through healing and recovery to embrace life anew and eventually – later in life than most men do – father two sons, Timothy and Brendan, and find lasting love.

Chapter 10

Laura Berry

The first-born daughter to Michael and Vivian Berry, Laura fondly remembers the early years with her parents. Eventually, she grew into a unique position that allowed her to know her father on another level, as a partner in his law firm – Berry, Francis, Seifman, Salamey & Harris. Laura's married name at the time was Harris.

The family's first house after leaving Canterbury in the South End was on Bingham in East Dearborn, not far from Fordson High School. Not very long after that, they moved to a house on Jim Daly [now Beech Daly], which was a dirt road. It dead-ended into farmland, and across the street from the Berry house was a farm with a lot of acreage and woods. On the same side of the street as the Berry's house

Laura Berry

were four homes. Laura was only five or six at the time.

"My dad bought me a dog, and I remember it chasing me around the yard. Some boys down the street that were a good bit older than I was picked on me a lot and threw me into a shallow pond. Dad was quite up-

119

set, so he called the boys' mother, and her response was not 'I'm sorry' but 'Boys will be boys.'

"Dad called a couple of his cousins and said, 'You need to talk to these boys.' I guess to them, talking was hitting or pushing them around, as if to say, 'touch her again, something more serious will happen to you.'

They were roughed up just enough to know that these bigger boys would come after them again, if necessary. The mother was quite upset and called my dad, who, of course, said only, 'Boys will be boys.' They never bothered me again.

Michael was and still is a very protective father. "If we were sick, he became extremely protective, making sure we went to the doctor. He would always ask, 'Well, what can I buy you?' You know - the strong mind-body connection. "

Michael's strictness was a trait that would be echoed later by Laura's sisters, but they all acknowledge he was lovingly strict. "We were a little slow in that we never quite figured out when Dad would get angry at us for misbehaving and take off his belt that he would hit us. We just knew that whenever he took off his belt, we'd better straighten up. As we grew older, we talked about that and laughed. We never figured out that he would never hit us, and he didn't, but we straightened out.

Being the eldest, Laura became the parental training ground and so received some stricter rules that Michael later relaxed a bit for the other girls. "When I was in junior high, I had a very short amount of time to get home from school, and I think this stemmed from his concern that something could happen to me. He did this with my sisters, too, but as we got a little older, he was less strict. We would still have to get permission, if we wanted to go outside the rules he set down for us.

"My mother would be supportive of my father, in that she would say, 'Call your father and ask him.' One time, I went with my friends to a little café on Telegraph Road. I had talked to my mother about this place where my friends often went, and I really felt badly that I couldn't go. One day, I went. A few minutes after I arrived there, my mother came and I had to go home, so I never did that again.

"I challenged my parents a bit, but not very much. I was not allowed to date until I was 16, although my friends were dating at 14 and 15, so that was difficult to go through. He always wanted us to dress respectfully. We did, although during the times when girls were wearing shorter skirts, I remember a couple of times rolling my skirt up so it would be at my knees instead of two or three inches below my knees."

Michael expected certain things of his girls. They had to do their homework first each afternoon, and when they brought home report cards, he would commend them for doing a good job, but always challenge them to do better. "So we always had that carrot out in front of us, so we would strive harder and harder. That really helped us later in life, because we all became a little competitive, not necessarily with each other but in our careers."

Laura believes that the successes that she and her siblings have enjoyed are directly related to their mother and father, and particularly their father's encouragement to be the best they could be.

Michael gave his daughters a belief in respect for everyone, respect for all ethnic groups and all religions. He made diversity popular with them long before it became what it is today. They knew that, being Lebanese, English, Irish, Scotch, and German, they were a Heinz 57 variety family, and he instilled in them pride in their heritage.

When Laura was in junior high, she was the only Muslim student, and later at Dearborn High School, she was the only Arab Muslim in the student body. "I took a class in which we studied the five major religions, and I did a report on Islam. It was very interesting. I was going to say one of our prayers, which we called the *fatiha*, as part of my report, so I started giving my report. Then I said I was going to say a prayer in Arabic. As I began to say it, some of the kids started snickering. I know it was a strange language for them, but then when I saw the teacher laughing, I was really hurt.

"Something interesting resulted from that, however. At that time, I had 13 warts on my hands and a large one on the middle finger of my right hand. After that report, we were to go to gym class. There, we would sit in rows, which the teacher called squads. This was at Bryant School, 6th grade. The girl behind me started talking about warts. She had two on one hand. She told me to look at her warts. As kids would do, I responded, 'That's nothing. You ought to see mine.' I extended both hands to show her. Remember this was in the class immediately following my report on Islam. To my complete shock, there were no warts on my hands!

"I was actually frightened. I called my parents right away. I believe it was a gift. God said not to be afraid of being religious. That's how my family and I interpreted that experience."

Laura knew she was different, but she never hid the fact that she was Muslim. Nor did she act like she was better than anyone else, because she was different. Her parents – especially Michael – fostered that line of thinking.

"I remember one girl, who had been my friend for a fair period of time, saying to me, 'My parents said that I can't hang around with you anymore. I can't play with you anymore.' I asked her why, because we were friends and had never had any arguments.

"She said it was because I was a foreigner. No, I told her, I am not a foreigner, but she said I was because I was from Lebanon. I explained that my grandparents were from Lebanon, but my parents and I were born in the United States, so I'm not a foreigner. Besides, I told her, there is nothing wrong with that.

"Then I asked her, 'Were you born here and were your parents born here?' She said yes, that she was Polish, but her grandparents were born in Poland. I concluded that she was as much a foreigner as I was."

Michael helped the girls understand that the differences in others did not make them inferior to them, but gave them other facets that they could enjoy. That was a very important and strong belief that is very helpful today. "I feel that everyone is my brother or sister. We're all people and we're all here for the same reason. That is from my father. That is what he taught us."

Michael encouraged the girls to follow what Islam really is, a religion of peace and one that teaches kindness and goodness. "Dad never made us pray five times a day, but we should pray. I remember praying at night. My mother was raised a Protestant, but she converted to Islam, and she prayed. She was able to make the transition.

"Dad wasn't real strict, but he encouraged us to have feelings from the heart, be a good person, and do the right thing. So, from that standpoint, he wanted us to be good Muslims. Also, there were dietary restrictions; we did not eat pork or drink alcohol.

"As an adult, I attend the mosque every Friday. I do not say the five daily prayers that the religion instructs, but I combine prayers. I'll say a prayer in the morning and one at night. I don't cover; I think that's more of a personal choice. I believe the intentions in my heart are good. I try to be a loving, kind person.

"I left the law because of stress and heart palpitations, and because it required me to be a person that goes against my nature. I am a very soft person, and one needs to be harder to practice law. I put that hat on when I practiced, but I just didn't like it. It just wasn't me."

Laura will always remember her father as a very kind man, helping a lot of people in a variety of ways. One time, in particular, stands out in her memory.

"When I was 11 or 12, I had a little white poodle named Fluffy that I loved dearly. My sisters and I were playing baseball in the backyard. I was pitching, and as my sister raised the bat, she accidentally hit Fluffy in the head. Dad rushed the dog to the veterinary clinic and later found out that she died.

"I was heartbroken. I went to bed but could not sleep, because I was crying. At about 11 p.m. my father called to me. I went to the top of the stairs with tears streaming down my face. He had his suit jacket on, and out of it popped the little white head of another dog that looked just like Fluffy! He had looked in the newspaper and talked to some people, even though it was late at night. He absolutely was determined to find the right dog and give it to me, because he could not stand to see me hurting. He did things like that, just kind and very loving things."

Michael's sense of humor and practical joking played out in places like Rotary Club, but the family also witnessed it. "Every once in a while, he would play a joke on us. I remember when we were watching the Beatles or some famous rock group on television, he would say, 'I can't believe they pay money to see these people.' Next thing we knew, he had bought a guitar, put on one of my mother's hairpieces, and started playing the guitar. He did it only once, but it brought laughter for years afterward, every time we remembered it."

Michael's love of cars captivated his girls and their friends. When Laura was 16, Michael had several cars in his collection of classics, and he let Laura drive them. She had a Corvette and other cars of her own. "Sometimes Mike drove me to school in a race car, and that was fun. Dad was more like a big brother when he was in that mode."

Having a Corvette attracted the boys, and one in particular showed great interest in Laura's. "When I found out he liked me because of my car, I went home and cried. I told my father I wanted a VW, because then a boy would like me for me. He consoled me. In comforting me, he made me realize that it was the boy's problem, that I had a lot to offer. It really didn't matter, he said, what kind of car I drove, what was in my heart was important, and there would always be people whose feelings I couldn't control. That made sense to me, although I was still hurting.

"He tried so hard to comfort my sisters and me at various times when we were growing up, so that we wouldn't have unhappy memories. He was very good about that.

"Dad liked to race – I probably shouldn't be telling this – but we'd go to the drive-ins when they were popular and Dad would rev his engine. Somebody would come out, and then he'd race on Telegraph Road. I think he didn't realize it was a dangerous sport. My friends always thought Dad was really cool, because he could be like one of our friends, as well, but I had to make sure I did things right and not get into trouble."

Laura remembered a time, when she was 16 or 17, and she was driving her girlfriends to the library in Dearborn. The three girls were in the front seat and, as teenagers would do, they were listening to the radio and bouncing around to the music. She noticed a sign at the corner of Michigan and Outer Drive and thought it said $500 fine for throwing trash on the highway. She turned and continued on Outer Drive, bopping to the music with her friends.

"The next thing we know a police car is behind us with lights flashing, so I pulled over. Truly I did not know what I had done. Unfortunately, the sign I saw said 'right turn on left after stop'. Of course, I did not stop; I was also going seven miles over the speed limit.

"Contrary to what my father had always told me, I didn't have my driver's license with me. When the officer asked me for my license, I couldn't produce it, and I told him about the sign. I doubt that he believed me. He asked if I knew that I was speeding. Finally, he said, 'I'm going to follow you home.' I was devastated, because I was fearful of my father finding out, because it would mean I let him down. It was just terrible."

The police followed Laura home, and one officer held her by the arm as he walked her to the front door. Michael answered the door. The officers looked at Michael, then at Laura and said, "Hi, Mike. I didn't know this was your daughter."

"That was the worst thing that could have happened. They sat down and talked to my father and made me go into another room. I'm sure in retrospect they talked about how they were going to frighten me.

"Finally, they called me in and told me that driving is dangerous and I should pay attention to signs and not go over the speed limit. They said they could give me tickets, but they didn't. I was a pretty obedient child, on the whole. After they left was the most fearful time. I knew I had disappointed my Dad."

Vivian was a homebody, very soft spoken and very kind. "I liked that they would go out and enjoy life. Mom always had her hair done on Fridays, and every Friday and Saturday night, Mom and Dad would go out. He really cherished her."

Michael is a very good cook, and Laura remembers that on Sundays, he would cook dinner when the girls were younger. He was famous for his leg of lamb and also something that his mother made of liver and assorted spices, called "goop". Back then, folks did not think about things like cholesterol; the family just knew it was delicious.

The girls would join Michael in the kitchen to help out. "Dad would say, 'Laura, peel an onion; Gail, chop up green peppers; Carol, do this, and Cindi, do that.' We'd all put our chopped up items in little bowls, like we had seen cooks do on TV. It was a lot of fun, because Dad made us feel that we were part of cooking. We didn't like the cleaning up part afterwards, however." He made each girl feel special; Laura, he said, made the best apple pie.

Family vacations were exciting times for the girls. "One time, Dad took us by train to California. Other times, we visited Florida, French Lick, Indiana, Greenbriar, West Virginia, and Washington, D. C. He took us to a lot of historical places, as well as some luxurious ones. I'm sure in his mind a lot of those choices went back to his upbringing. He didn't get to go anywhere in the United States as a child, so he wanted us to have that advantage.

"He's very proud of this country and of his Lebanese heritage. He and my mother wanted us to have the same feelings, and I believe they succeeded."

Laura, as well as two of her sisters, was a late bloomer. She started college, married, had a child, divorced, and married again. She returned to school late in life.

"From the time I started to the time I finished, it took 19 years. Then I went to Detroit College of Law, just as Dad had done. I don't know if he would admit it, but he tried to talk me out of going into law, because he knew my personality and thought I would be too shy."

She makes no bones about the ease of joining her father's law firm after she passed the Bar. "It was great because Dad and the other partners were very welcoming. They took me under their wings, even taking me to lunch with them. It gave me the opportunity to learn a lot faster than others would have learned. I was still shy, however, but my father dealt with that head-on."

Being the law firm representing the City of Romulus meant they had to do prosecution work, too. When Laura first joined the firm, Michael had her handle the prosecution, which meant she would have to participate in numerous trials, both jury and bench.

"I was frightened to death! I remember going in with a terrible headache due to the stress of having to speak in public. I prepared everything I would have to say and then I practically read it, barely looking up, I was so frightened.

"As I progressed from having to do these trials, I came to that point – rather quickly because of the frequency – of feeling comfortable enough to just jot down the major points, walk in front of the jury, and talk to the judge. I realized that people are people and just because they are in a position of power, I wouldn't die if I made a mistake.

"If Dad had not tossed me into the ocean to see if I could swim, I might not have succeeded in doing jury and bench trials after that. I gained a lot of confidence from those experiences. Dad knew what he was doing when he gave me a push. It was the best thing he could have done to me to get me over my fear of public speaking.

"After that, I learned from watching him. He could take two very divergent positions. People would come to him for resolution of a problem, and he would listen to both sides and find a creative solution based on something that both parties had in common. They both walked away with something positive. He was very good at making creative solutions."

Laura served as city attorney for the City of Dearborn Heights. When she started in that position, the mayor's father was mayor when Michael was the Dearborn Heights Township attorney; it had turned around completely some 30 years later. People still remembered Michael, and loved him, as they learned to love Laura. It was a great experience for her.

"The Mayor of Dearborn Heights cried when I left. She really liked me, and I liked everyone in city government there. The city council didn't want me to leave, but I stayed on until they found a replacement. I felt that my decision was the right one for me. I'm back to being the real me, and I'm happy."

"I believe I owe everything to my father. He's a magnificent person. I cannot express how much I love him and hold him in high esteem. He's always been careful about treating us girls equally. If he gave one something, he gave us all. He wanted to make sure none of us felt slighted, that we felt loved equally."

Chapter 11

Carol Berry Ward

One of Carol's fondest memories takes her back to when she was eight years old, when she was then one of three sisters. "Every summer we would go to my dad's office in downtown Detroit for the whole day. Each sister took turns, so each of us got her turn for Daddy time. We had breakfast with Dad and maybe one of his partners, Thornton Hopson or John Francis. Then we would go to the office and play on the typewriter or Mr. Hopson's adding machine.

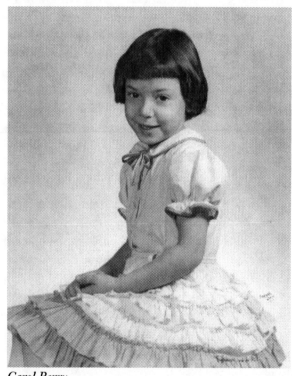

Carol Berry

"I would scribble on legal pads, pretending I was taking dictation. Then we would go out to lunch with Dad's secretary – Frances was our favorite, but she got married and moved away. After lunch, we would spend the afternoon shopping. It was such a fun day. These summer office visits went on for at least five years."

Carol echoes her sister Laura's thoughts about their father's strictness. "I don't know why he was so strict, but we weren't allowed to date until we were 16. He bent the rules for me once for a special date to the prom, but then it was no more special favors for six months!"

Vivian knew how strict Michael was with the girls, and she tried to soften the rules at times. "She thought his strictness was a little unreasonable. One time, I don't recall what age I was, but I was on the telephone. My father asked me who I was talking to, and I said it was a boy by such-and-such a name. Dad pulled the plug on the phone! I was so angry at him. He just didn't want me talking to boys."

Curfews for the girls were earlier than those of their friends, and sleepovers, which were very popular then, were not permitted. "A couple of times, my friends had pajama parties, and I was allowed to go to the party first, but then I had to come home."

Highlighted in Carol's early memories are the great vacations the family took. "We went to Montreal, and in the hotel where we were staying, Chubby Checker was performing at the height of his popular rock-n-roll song and dance, the Twist. I got up on stage and danced the Twist with Chubby Checker."

Another memorable trip was to Beirut, when it was the Riviera of the Middle East. "It was so gorgeous," Carol recalls. "We visited Tibnin, where my grandparents were from, and Dad showed me the fortress where he played when he went there as a kid."

Carol remembers what a wonderful cook her father is. "But when he cooks, he messes up the whole kitchen. He didn't have to do any of the clean up; we had to do that. That would infuriate me. He depended on us for that. My mother was wonderful and did so much. She lived solely for her man and her kids."

Carol attended Western Michigan University. Three semesters into her term there, she met Tim Ward, and they decided to get married. "I remember coming home to tell my dad. I was a little nervous. My mother knew in advance what I was going to tell him. We were talking at lunch, and Dad said, 'The next thing you know she'll tell me she wants to get married.'

"I said, 'Well, Dad...' and he slapped the table in the restaurant and said, 'She does! She does!' He was so upset, but once he met Tim, he was more amenable.

After their July 1969 wedding, Carol and Tim moved to Arlington

Heights, Illinois, Tim's hometown. "We stayed there for a year. I worked and went to junior college, and then we came back to Michigan. I worked while Tim finished his degree in business management."

Tim then worked for Wayne County, starting with an entry-level position and then taking Civil Service tests to move up the ladder. He eventually became Managing Director of Detroit Metropolitan Airport, but resigned on principle when undue pressure was put on him to sell tickets to political fundraisers, an inappropriate activity for one negotiating county contracts.

After entertaining three opportunities to manage airports in Seattle, Jacksonville, Florida, and Austin, Texas, Tim decided to accept the offer in Austin. He and Carol lived there for four years. During that time, he handled the negotiations for a new airport in Austin, attending all the meetings with subdivision owners and residents to allay their fears. He was in constant contact with the FAA, and the people there took a liking to Tim.

He received the first license issued for a new airport since World War II. "Then came the election for the council, which controls the airport," explains Michael. "Tim met with one council member who wanted his sister's baked goods to be sold at the airport. Tim said he could not authorize that, because even before he arrived in Austin, the council had signed 20-year contracts with another bakery, and the council had to approve anyone who came in to sell similar products."

Every week the man put pressure on Tim, and one day he decided he had had enough. He called Michael. "I quit, Dad." He assured Michael that he had enough money to carry the family through until he found another job.

Tim called the FAA and let them know he was available. "Lo and behold," Michael says, "shortly afterward, H. Ross Perot, Jr. contacted the FAA, looking for manager to run his new Fort Worth Alliance Airport. It's known as the world's first purely industrial airport.

"Tim was there at the right time. Perot contacted Tim, but he would not offer him a job until he met Tim's family; it's his policy. So Perot flew his helicopter from Dallas to Austin, picked up Carol and their two sons – Jason and Michael – and took them to Dallas. They had dinner together, and the next day he hired Tim."

Today, Tim still works for H. Ross Perot, Jr. He and Carol live in Colleyville, Texas.

Chapter 12

Gail Berry

In any family in which one parent works long hours away from the home, the other parent fills in for the children. And so it was with Michael and Vivian. Gail remembers that her father's absence from home due to his active law prac-tice and role in poli-tics made her – and her sisters – closer to their mother; in fact, Gail was prob-ably closer to her mother because they spent a lot of time together. "We used to talk a lot. I felt I could tell her just about anything." It became more of a friendship than a mother-daughter relationship.

Gail Berry

"Vivian was a sweetheart, an an-gel," she says. "She was probably a lit-tle on the innocent side, but she was always there for me. If I broke up with a boyfriend, she would console me. We used to watch old movies together in the summers. She had a quiet, reserved personal-ity, but she had some friends, including the woman who lived across the street from us.

"She was German, English, Irish, and Scottish, and an excellent cook. She made some German dishes, but she learned to cook Lebanese style, and she was excellent at that, which is not easy to do. We had family dinner at the table. No TV. No radio."

The family had lived their entire lives in the Dearborn area, so everyone was excited to move to Plymouth Township in 1971. That was Gail's first year in college. "I was living at Marygrove during the week and coming home on the weekends. It was an exciting time. My younger sister, Cindi, lived at home. She loved horses, but they were not my love."

Following Vivian's untimely death [Chapter 14], Gail became introverted. "I just was not going to show my emotions anymore," she recalls. "I was always shy and like my mother in that respect. The nuns at Marygrove were wonderful, absolutely wonderful. They were very helpful in those days."

Gail's life changed in other ways, too. "I think my mother's death changed me dramatically. I now keep a gun in the house, and I know how to use it and am comfortable with it. I'm not as trusting as I used to be. Prior to her death, I would have helped anybody. Not that I'm totally cold toward people now; it's just that I'm not going to put myself in a position of vulnerability. I have helped some people to a certain extent, but there is always that sense of caution."

Michael, Gail, and Cindi moved into the Dearborn Towers. "That was a big change for us, but it was a good transition," says Gail. "It was a very big change for me, because I kind of had to be the mother. I had to learn how to cook and do the laundry for the three of us."

That completed the summer of 1972. Then Gail returned to Marygrove on weekdays. She completed a four-year program and received her degree in philosophy.

When she was a junior, she became engaged to John Palazzolo. They both graduated at the same time, and after graduation, they married. Gail felt sad that he would never meet her mother.

As it turned out, Gail and Cindi were married on the same day in 1975. "We had two separate weddings and the same reception at Hillcrest Country Club in Macomb County. It was a huge wedding attended by 500 to 600 people. There were a lot of gate crashers, too."

Gail began working for Ford Credit. "John and I moved into an apartment on Inkster off of Cherry Hill. We lived there for one-and-a-half years and then we bought a house, the same house in Dearborn where I live today."

By the time Gail's marriage was experiencing a downturn, Cindi was pregnant with her first child. "I really wanted to have kids at that time in my life," says Gail, "so I told Cindi she was actually carrying my baby, and I thanked her for it. I'm real close to Kyle, her first-born. She's in law school in California now."

In 1984, Gail and John went through an amicable divorce. They remained close friends for a while, but then, as it often happens, they drifted apart.

Evaluating her father's personality, Gail turns to his life experiences. "In his law practice he has seen the ugliest sides of people and the best sides of people. One characteristic of my father would be his suspicious nature, always being on guard. That was part of his life, from the stand-point of his profession.

"I personally felt he was always suspicious of me, in terms of my activities when I was growing up. If I went out with my friends, he always wanted to know who I was going with, where I was going to go, what time was I leaving, and when would I be home. And, if I went anywhere else, I had to call and inform him. I thought he was overprotective. I knew I wasn't going to get into any trouble, but he didn't. That was the one thing that was a little choking at times.

"Then when boys started calling on me, they were afraid to come in, because Dad would act the attorney in quizzing them as to their intentions. He wanted to check their story out with mine, too.

"In hindsight, a lot of that strictness may have stemmed from the fact that he was not home a lot and that made it difficult for us to relate to him. It also brought out a rebellious side in me. I would take the opposite side of any stance my dad would take, deliberately. Sometimes it got me in trouble. We would have discussions, and he would get upset. I believe I did that on purpose, just to get some reaction from him, which gave me the feeling that he and I had a relationship. I would be passionate in the stance I took."

If there was a character flaw in Michael, Gail felt it was from a family standpoint, not a community one. "He was always so ready to help anybody else, but he wasn't there for us. I think because he was so tied up in his work during our growing up years, he didn't know how to express his love for us other than by giving us gifts. My mother was very affectionate, and since her death, he became much affectionate and has grown a lot, too. You might say we forced him to be affectionate."

On a more humorous note, Gail remembers when Michael taught her how to drive a stick shift on his red Ferrari, which was one of only 12 of its kind in the world. "These cars are built for a man to drive," Gail says, "certainly someone taller than I am. I didn't want to learn on this particular car, but I had no choice. So, in order to stick the clutch in, I had to scoot down, at which point, I could not see over the steering wheel. I scooted back up when I let the clutch up and put the gas on.

"Every time I stalled the car, my dad went ballistic. I just couldn't wait until I got home. I told him, 'I'm going to ask my friend to teach me on their VW beetle.' Never let someone try to teach you on a car they adore. I was terrified, and it was a horrendous experience…for me and for my dad, especially grinding the gears!"

The best part of that kind of memory is being able to look back and laugh.

Chapter 13

Cindi Berry LaCroix, DVM

Some experiences in our childhood lay the groundwork for a lifelong career. In Cindi Berry LaCroix's case, it was the love of horses that she shared with her father that led her to become a horse veterinarian.

"When our family went to Lebanon, that's when I decided I wanted a white Arabian horse," she recalls. "I was eight or nine years old. I loved being with my father when he went to see horses; I loved the smell of the barns and the beautiful horses."

Cindi finally got her first white Arabian, Myameer, whose mare was Fancy Lady bred to Diamond. The rest, as the saying goes, is history. "I always wanted to be a veterinarian; and now I take care of horses exclusively."

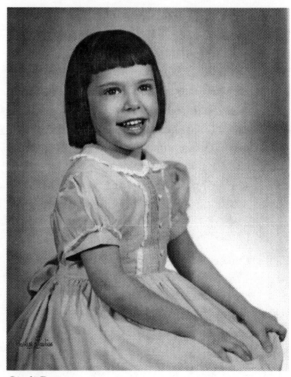

Cindi Berry

That would not have been the case if she had listened to medical advice. Cindi was diagnosed with rheumatoid arthritis when she was only six years old, and doctors later told her not to work with large animals.

Her sister Laura explains Cindi's determination. "She was not going to let her condition or the doctor's warnings deter her from doing what she really wanted to do. All the exercise she got from riding horses and showing them kept her limber, and she is limber, despite having three hip replacements. She's a very determined lady.

"She got treated a bit differently than her sisters did, in that she had to go through certain exercises when she was young. We all felt terrible that she had to go through that, and now I think she played that to her advantage a little when she got older.

"Above all she wanted a horse, and so she got a horse. I'm sure if all of us girls wanted horses, Dad would have given each of us our very own horse."

It wasn't just her father's love of horses that Cindi appreciated. "I adore the man. He's the most kind-hearted, generous person there is. My earliest memory was an incident that demonstrated how very honest he is. I remember a man meeting with my father, and the man lied to my father. I remember him getting very loud and yelling, 'Don't ever lie to me!' It was because he so rarely yelled that it made an impression on me as a young girl. It was my introduction to his honesty and his integrity."

While Michael didn't yell at the girls much, Cindi also experienced the strictness that her sisters knew. "Dad never did anything to make us feel afraid, but we didn't want to cross him. My mother was a sweetheart. If Dad wasn't at home, she let us do pretty much whatever we wanted to do. I never ever remember hearing her yell. Never. She and my father were madly in love with each other. I think her death was the only time I saw my father cry. Well, no, there was another time, at the last dinner we had before I moved to Arizona. He was all teary-eyed then, too."

After Vivian's death, Cindi grew closer to her father, because she was the only one living at home with him. Gail was there, too, but usually only on weekends.

Cindi graduated from Dearborn High School and married soon afterward to a young man, who had already graduated from college. The marriage did not last, and after the divorce, Cindi enrolled in the Veterinary Medicine Program at Michigan State University. She received her DVM degree in 1991 and set up her own veterinarian practice in Brighton.

In the course of her work, she met Raymond LaCroix, whose fam-

Michael Berry & daughter Cindi, 2003

ily owned a big Arabian horse farm in Metamora, Michigan. He is an Arabian horse trainer, so the match was, one might say, made in heaven. They moved to Scottsdale, Arizona in 2001.

"What started out to be a part-time practice," says Cindi, "quickly became full time with other veterinarians working for me. There are tons of horses out here! Now, I'm in solo practice, working exclusively with horses."

No discussion with the girls about their father would be complete without it eventually turning to his sense of humor or funny things that happened in the family.

"When we were little," Cindi recalls, "he used to tell us funny jungle stories and he would assume the voices of different animals. We all heard them when we were young and then the grandchildren would hear them and they all loved them. When my father was in Florida for half the year, my daughter Kyle, whom he adored, would have to call Dad every night before she went to bed, just so he could tell her another jungle story. Dad adores kids!"

Sometimes, though, kids can test our patience. "One time, we were at Cindi's house for a holiday dinner or maybe a birthday," says Laura. "Dad had a brand new Mercedes parked in the driveway. Cindi's son,

Daniel, about six years old at the time, was outside playing. After a while he came into the house with a brick in his hand. 'Hi, Papa,' he said. 'I washed your car for you.'

"Daniel had washed Dad's brand new car with a brick, pretending it was a sponge. Dad took it so well. He simply told him, 'That was really nice of you, but you should use a sponge.' Even though there were marks on his new car, Dad handled it very well. And now we all look back on it and laugh."

Cindi's three grown children from her first marriage are all highly ambitious and determined young adults. Kyle, Michael's first granddaughter, is pursuing her law degree at Pepperdine University in California; Daniel is studying environmental science at the University of Arizona, and Vivian Carol, named for her grandmother, is in her second year at the University of Arizona.

Chapter 14

Vivian

They seemed to be the perfect family: loving parents and respectful children. Michael Berry was a successful attorney and an admired politician, chairing the powerful Wayne County Road Commission. Vivian was the dutiful, loving wife, whom everyone admired. The four daughters – Laura, Carol, Gail, and Cindi – were their shining stars. With so much positive energy in one family, it is inconceivable that a dark cloud could find room to change their lives forever.

Vivian Weine Berry

"Mike had the perfect politician's marriage," the late Judge George Bashara recounted. "Vivian was a very sweet, very lovely person. She was not Lebanese, but she gave him due deference. She understood the Muslim way of living. Even though she was not a Muslim before she married him, she gave him free rein to do whatever he had to do in the world of politics. There were many nights when he did not come home, but she always faithfully waited for him. He was very close to her, and she was very close to him."

From 1968 to 1972, Michael concentrated on his law practice and his work at the Road Commission. In 1969, the family went to Florida for the winter. By then the girls were growing up, and he enrolled them in school there. They were all good students, which was a tribute to their strong and loving parental upbringing.

Having lived in the same home in Dearborn from 1957 to 1970, they decided to look for a new home. Jim Davey told Michael about some property in a rural area, and Michael purchased that 72-acre parcel. He started to put a road up to the top of the hill, where he wanted to build a house.

Then Jim found a property in Plymouth Township, and Michael and Vivian fell in love with it. There was a huge house, fairly modern for the times, with a lake on one side of the property. The family wanted to have a place large enough for a barn and a dozen horses.

Michael sold their house in West Dearborn, and the family moved into their new home in July 1971. "I started with 20 acres and wound up with 237. We had four or five horses, but they were not there yet, as I needed to build the barn.

"Just two of our daughters – Gail and Cindi – were living with us, as Laura and Carol had married and were on their own. We enrolled Cindi and I drove her to school in Plymouth, because we lived on North Territorial, which was rural at that time."

After a trip with the Chamber of Commerce, Michael returned home on May 8, 1972, his birthday. The family gathered that evening to celebrate, and the next morning, Michael left for work. It was a Thursday, when the Road Commission board held its regular meeting on the 7th floor of the City County Building.

Bette Misuraca remembers vividly the events of that morning. "Mike came out of the meeting and asked me to place a call to Vivian. It was between 9:30 and 10:00. I tried to call her but the line was busy. Another 45 minutes later, he came out and said, 'Did you forget the phone call?' I said, 'No, Mr. Berry. I've been calling but the line has been busy.' So as he was going back to the meeting he said, 'I don't know where she could be or who she could be talking to that long.'

"He came back again, all through the board meeting. Then he told me to call his daughter, Gail, at school."

Bette noticed the concern Michael demonstrated about Vivian, even before he knew there was a problem. He just wanted to check in with her. "It was my insight into how very intent he was on trying to reach her to make sure she was all right. He must have had a premonition, because he kept coming out to see if she had called."

Miles away from the Road Commission meeting, Michael's 18-year-old daughter, Gail, was attending a summer class at Schoolcraft College. She had no idea her life was about to change forever.

"A student in my class asked me to stop and have coffee with him, and so we did," she remembers. "We had a nice chat, and then I headed home. That was around noon. When I pulled up, I noticed my sister Carol's car in the driveway, and I wondered what was going on. She wasn't living there, as she was already married. As soon as I pulled up, she came up to me. She was really shaken up.

"She told me Dad had been trying to reach our mother, but she didn't answer the phone. The car was in the garage. Carol couldn't get in the house, because the door was locked and she didn't have a key. She asked me if I had a key, and I said, yes. The funniest thing was I believe I was ordained to find our mother, because I was the calmest of the four girls. Although I always kept my house key in the front right pocket of my jeans, that day I forgot where it was and I couldn't find it.

"Carol said she would go to town and call Dad and tell him we couldn't get in the house. As soon as she left, I remembered where I put my key – just where I always kept it! I put the key in the lock but I still could not get in, because the deadbolt lock was on. I went around to the front of the house, and the door was ajar. I knew instinctively something was wrong. I opened the door cautiously and went inside. In the dining room, I saw one of Mom's loafers and on the dining room table was the phone and the telephone book opened to auto repairs. That didn't look right. I thought to myself, 'Gail, be careful, because you don't know what's going on.'

"The phone rang. I answered it. It was Dad. 'You found her?' he asked. 'Is everything okay?'

"I told him I hadn't found her yet, so I told him to hold on a minute. I put the phone down. Our house was split level, and I had already checked the upper level, so I went down the stairs to the lower level. As I rounded the corner of the stairs, to my right, I saw that the garage was open. I had a very strong sensation that that was where I would find her.

I saw what I saw. I started screaming. I ran up the stairs screaming, and yet while I was doing that, I immediately questioned what I had seen. Right then and there, disbelief started setting in. I'm not really sure what I saw. I remember details right up to the moment I saw her and right after that, but it's that picture of her that I cannot bring to mind, and I'm so thankful for that. I never want to remember that scene."

Finally, back at the Road Commission office, a call came for Michael. "Before I knew who was calling, I could tell by the expression on Bette's face that something was wrong," he recalls. "When I answered the phone, it was Gail. She was literally screaming, 'She's dead! She's dead!'"

Michael said, "Calm down, calm down. What is it, honey? What are you talking about?"

"My mother's dead," Gail sobbed.

"How can you tell? Call 411 and get the police out there to check her pulse!" Michael told her.

"I can't. I can't. She's bloody all over. She's dead!"

After Michael hung up the phone to rush home, Gail wondered if the killer was still in the house. "I went to the kitchen to pull a knife out of the drawer. I thought, no, I'm not going to do what he did, so I put the knife back in the drawer. I waited out by the door until the police arrived.

"Cindi arrived. Carol had picked her up at school. Cindi ran in front of the police and asked, 'Where's Mom?' I told her that Mom was in the garage and she shouldn't go in there. She had to go see for herself.

"Later, I was sitting in the dining room, telling the police what I knew. Cindi came running up the stairs and fell on her knees in front of me, screaming and screaming and screaming. I remember smacking her to make her stop. Then, she broke down crying. I remember the police saying something about me being in shock."

Meanwhile, an elderly man, Bob, who had been in practice for 15 years before Michael joined the commission, and Michael got into his car. "I drove at speeds from 70 to 90 mph," says Michael, "and Bob was frightened to death the whole time. He wanted to come with me, and it's a good thing he did.

"When I got there, the ambulance had already taken away Vivian's body. The police were there, and I found my daughters. I just slumped in disbelief on the grass in front of the house. I don't remember much of what anyone around me said; I was surely in shock. Bill Lucas was sheriff at the time, and he said he would do everything he could to find the guilty party, and he did."

"Dad had us sit in the backseat of his car and not go back into the house," says Gail. "I remember telling somebody to go and tell Laura. Don't call her, I said, because she would totally freak out. Laura is a very fragile person, especially with death. I was afraid she would have gotten into an accident in her rush to get out to the house. I kept telling people, 'Go get Laura. Don't let her drive.' She lived and worked in Dearborn. Unfortunately, no one called her, and she learned the news on the radio. That was an awful way for her to find out."

The suspect was a 17-year-old boy whose parents were in the Livonia school system, one as a principal and the other, a teacher. This boy – as told to Michael by others that had never talked to the boy – had at an early age of 14 shown signs of propensity for violence. He had taken the eye out of a classmate with a piece of steel.

Apparently there had been a complaint called in to the police that a young man was going from farmhouse to farmhouse asking to use the telephone. That tied in with the fact that the Yellow Pages directory was open on the dining room table at the Berry home. Apparently the kid had told Vivian he was having transmission problems with his car and needed to call for service.

The police checked with other neighbors, and the boy had stopped at their homes, too, but a big dog deterred him, and at the other home, the husband answered the door and didn't like the kid's appearance.

"On top of that evidence, the police found a key in the boy's possession," explains Michael. "Our house had a double lock with a key on the inside of the house. He had put the dead bolt on and taken the key with him. The police found it in his pocket. He had evidently tried to rob Vivian. She ran from him, while he was stabbing her. She collapsed and died in the garage of at least 72 stab wounds, according to the coroner. This was the fury and intensity of this young man. I couldn't go down to identify the body, but my two brothers, Henry and Lindy, went to the morgue and identified her for me."

Michael and the girls were in the courtroom during part of the trial. "I had the coroner's report with me when I went to court and as a result I momentarily lost my senses, because believe it or not I was contemplating killing the boy when I saw the sheriff deputy's holster with the gun in it. This was on the 18th floor of the City County building, before Judge Bowles. The prosecutor was a very highly competent attorney from

Grosse Pointe. Several years later we had lunch and reviewed what had happened (the trial).

"At the time, I nearly committed murder myself. The gun was available. It looked very much available in the holster. It would not have been easy but I would have gotten access to it, because he was standing right next to me. There was no reason for the deputy to think that I would contemplate such a move. I know I could have gotten the gun and blown the kid's head off, because he was standing right there, handcuffed.

"At the same time that crossed my mind – believe it or not – I looked at this kid and thought, if you make this move, Mike, you're going to be right where he is, and you have your daughters to take care of. You would be doing a disservice to the rest of the family to satisfy this urge. So I immediately walked away and went into the courtroom and sat down.

"When I had to testify, I told only what I knew...the phone call, where I was, where I had been the day before the murder. During my testimony, Judge Bowles broke down and had to leave the bench. I broke down, and so did many of the jurors. Of course, the story was all over the papers, too much so."

The outcome of the trial was that the young man was convicted of first degree murder. He was given a life sentence without the possibility of parole.

The family never returned to their house in Plymouth again. Herschel Hogan and his wife went to the house and cleaned up the blood. Many friends volunteered to get the furniture and personal belongings out of the house. It was gratifying to Michael and his family to have such outpouring of sympathy and compassion.

The funeral was held at the Islamic Center with one of the largest crowds ever. "I don't know if it was because of who we were or because of the publicity given to the crime at the time," says Michael. "The governor came, as well as a lot of dignitaries and labor leaders, Bard Young, my mentor, especially; he was really a first class guy. Bard had one of his aides, Clarence Contratto, constantly with me throughout that period and I remember all the charitable things they did for me and my family.

"It was the low point of my life, and I would like to add that many a night after the funeral I contemplated suicide, but I always came to the conclusion my children came first.

"I never went back to the house, not even when I sold it. The day she died, my dream of having a place where we would live out the rest of our years was shattered."

Michael and the two girls stayed for a week at his brother's home and after that, Jim Davey secured an apartment in the Dearborn Towers in West Dearborn. They stayed there for a few months.

In July of 1972, Labor sought to have Michael run for the office of chairman of the State Democratic Party. They called him to meet them at the Sheik Café in downtown Detroit. There were a number of people in attendance, including Bard Young, Doug Fraser, and many of the leadership of the UAW, plus a couple of persons from outside Wayne County that were leaders in their particular districts.

"The consensus had been that I had the greatest number of votes pretty much garnered to elect me on the first roll call, if everybody abided by their decision. They wanted to know from me at that time if I was still gung-ho to run for the office of state chairman.

"They were wondering because of the lingering effect of the tragedy of my wife's murder. It didn't require much thought on my part. I had to weigh my responsibility to my two remaining daughters who were at home. Gail was 18, going on 19; she was attending Marygrove College. Cindi must have been 14. At that age they needed somebody at home. I decided that in order to campaign for that office, in order to do the job as state chairman, I would have to cover the state of Michigan. I knew that it would mean leaving the two girls alone in the house, so I decided immediately that I would not run for that office."

As a matter of fact, Michael did not go to the state convention that year. He continued going to work in his law practice and at the Road Commission, but he dropped out of the political arena in any official capacity.

"I asked the girls to take on the duty of finding a home, a place to for us to live. They found a house at the corner of Fairmont and Silvery Lane in West Dearborn and we moved there in the winter of 1972.

"Fairmont runs along the northerly end of the golf course. It is a lovely street, and our new home gave us an opportunity to move on with our lives, although one never really forgets such an enormous tragic event, especially when it comes so unexpectedly, without notice or provocation."

Chapter 15

The sting of family tragedy lingers long after the tears have dried. It leaves a hole that takes time to fill, but never quite succeeds in doing so. Some people leave indelible footprints in our lives, and Vivian surely did so to those she loved and those who loved her.

Getting on with one's life is challenging, but when others depend on your strength, you muster the courage to go on and try to make life seem normal again. That's the way Michael moved forward. He continued his law practice and work at the Wayne County Road Commission. He and the girls started life in a new home and carved out a new slate of memories as a smaller family, forever changed.

Michael's friends, especially Bette Misuraca at the Road Commission and Dottie Engle, Congressman Dingell's secretary, played a significant role in helping him with the girls. His best friends, Bard Young, Sam Zehra, and Clarence Contratto were there for him when he needed them.

Although dating and remarriage was not foremost in Michael's mind, after six years his desire and need for female companionship grew stronger. He is not one to live life alone. He didn't have to look far to find a woman who made him laugh and enjoyed many of his interests, particularly horses.

Diane Wazney was born in the South End. Her mother went back to Tibnin when she was a kid, grew up there and married Diane's father. They immigrated to the United States and settled in the South End. "People from many other countries lived in the South End because they couldn't afford to live anywhere else. They lived in the shadow of the Ford Motor Company, and the men all carried their black lunch buckets, like Michael's father, as a sign of pride, as if to announce, 'I work at Ford.' Even old Henry himself carried a lunch bucket.

"Many years earlier, Mike's mother used to ask me, 'Why don't you marry my son?' I always said, 'Oh, no, nobody can live with him.' You have to be a strong person to be married to Michael, so you don't get swallowed up."

"My brother was good friends with one of Mike's brothers, and I was close to one of his sisters," Diane reflects. "We've known each other all our lives. Things evolved and we ended up getting married."

In 1977, they were married. Alex Balooly, owner of Topinka's, held the reception. "They used to come to Topinka's all the time," Alex said. "We became very close. To me, he's like family. Any time you need anything; you just pick up the phone and call him. He always knows who to call. A lot of times people, especially our people, expect you to bend the law, but Mike's not that kind of guy. He goes by the book."

When people say to Diane how lucky Michael is, he has it made, she tells them, "Yes, he was born into this position in life, right? Is that what you think?" They say, yeah, right. "Then I explain that it wasn't luck at all; it was hard work. He didn't have any advantages. His parents couldn't even read and write much. Our parents were all immigrants.

"Mike never forgot where he came from. He never forgot the old friends from the neighborhood. You don't leave and say, 'I don't know them anymore.' We still know all of them. What's good about both of us, we know the same characters by their nicknames. We speak the same language. It made it easier in our relationship.

"Mike didn't have an environment of education at home, but he went ahead and educated himself. When Mike went to school, he didn't have much money, and he couldn't afford to eat much. He would watch his friends around him eating, and he would have only a candy bar, but he was hungry. He went through law school that way, living pretty much on candy bars. Despite that, he finished law school and became one of the most capable lawyers in the State of Michigan."

Michael's daughters and Diane knew each other long before Diane and Michael got married. "Vivian was a sweet, very nice lady. One time we were at the mosque, and Michael asked my mother and me for a ride home...in Plymouth Township. I had his mother with me, so we drove him all the way home. We saw his house for the first time.

"Now, I never fear anything, but when I saw the house, I said to Vivian, 'Aren't you afraid out here? A person could get killed out here and no one would ever know about it. You can't see the road.' A few months later she was killed. It was a terrible tragedy.

"Much later, after Michael and I started dating, Gail sat in my kitchen and told me the whole story. She was shaking, but she had to get it out.

"I never thought of going out with Michael for a long time. He was family to me. The girls did well after their mother died, although it is usually more difficult for girls to lose their mother, but Michael tried to serve in both capacities."

Common backgrounds and upbringing made the transition from second cousins to spouses relatively easy. "We went together for a long time – four or five years – and we had a lot of fun. We were married 11 or 12 years. People don't understand why we are friends, but we were friends before; we can be friends after. Life is too short to be angry."

Their love of horses kept the marriage alive. "We both loved our horses. We loved owning them, going to horse auctions, and racing horses. Over the 11 years that we were married, we bought some quite famous horses that did well."

They enjoyed winning, but sometimes life put that into perspective in penetrating ways. Diane tells this story. "We were coming back from New York after a big race. We got off at a certain exit, and we saw a man, woman, boy, and girl with everything they owned in their suitcases. I was driving, so as we went up the ramp, I stopped the car. Michael gave them money, and the boy said, 'Thank you, mister. Thank you.' Well, I started to cry, and Michael started to cry. 'Why are we crying?' we asked ourselves.

"Then Michael said, 'This is terrible that people are like this. Who's going to take care of them tomorrow?' We had just won a race, and I concluded that we were indeed lucky.

"Michael is a really sensitive guy. He cries at movies just like a kid."

Political differences added sparks to Diane and Michael's relationship. She is a Republican; Michael is a highly influential Democrat. She worked for Orville Hubbard; he campaigned for his recall. Her family's friendship eventually healed that rift, and Michael and Orville became friends.

Diane was never one to mince words or hold back her feelings, and Michael would nudge her under the table to put her outspokenness in check. "I have a bad habit," she admits. "If I want to say something, I say it, even if it means losing millions. So what? If you're wrong, you're wrong and I'm going to tell you. That was my mother's way – take the straight road; don't waffle here and there." One story clearly demonstrates this point.

"We were at a St. Jude's annual dinner in Florida," Diane recalls. "Michael was on the board, so we knew these people. At that time, the

Syrians were coming into Lebanon and the civil war was going on. A guy who sat at our table had just returned from Lebanon. We asked, 'How is everything going?' He said, 'It's going all right for us. Most of the fighting is in the south, so I don't care, because they're all Muslims. They're killing them down there; they're not fighting in the north.'

"This was an Arab American speaking! I was ready to jump, and Michael nudged me under the table. This guy goes on and on. He didn't know we were Muslim. I was not satisfied with saying nothing. My style would have been to reach across the table and slap, slap, slap him. Michael's is to wait it out. I'd ask Michael, 'Why is this man getting away with this?' and he would say, 'Give me time.' There is no such thing as time in my life.

"Even on the Road Commission, when the *Detroit News* attacked Michael, he never cried civil rights. I used to tell him, 'When you're not chairman of the Road Commission anymore, a lot of these people will disappear. They come because they need something. When the next person takes control, they'll be over there. They're chameleons.

"I have a very cynical view of politicians on both sides of the aisle. And news people. Michael has nudged me so many times under the table, and the more he did, the madder I got. I called Joel Smith [the *Detroit News* writer who launched the attack on Michael] a whore. I told him, 'You have the nerve to sit and write this stuff and you want to have the last word. Give me a column, and I'll write the truth.' Michael kept nudging me under the table."

Diane and Michael loved horses and laughed often, but the undoing of their marriage was, ironically, communication. "Michael and I were never at a loss for words, but the phones interrupted our conversations so much, the only time I really got to talk to him was when we were in the car or on a trip somewhere. We could talk about anything and everything, but when he was around a telephone, he was constantly calling someone or taking a call. Once he told me he was going to have a phone put in the car, and I told him if he did that, I would divorce him. We had a lot of fights over that.

"Michael was in constant communication. That's what did us in. To me, the most important reason you get married is to have some companionship. We couldn't even sit through dinner. I'm not exaggerating. It was constant. In order to communicate with Michael, I wrote him a letter and sent it to his office. 'Why,' I asked, 'do I have difficulty communicating with you? Why don't you ever consider spending time with me? I'm not asking you for money or material things…just time. Is there something wrong with that? It means a person cares if they ask for your time.' It was like I was living alone, so I figured I might as well be single."

"We agreed on the divorce," Michael relates. "We were sitting with the family. We didn't have an argument; no one knew what we were doing. It was very civil. Our judicial friends said, 'We don't like to see this happen.' The law requires a minimum of 60 days for a divorce; it took 62 days for our divorce."

Michael and Diane remain very good friends. Their stories for this book were peppered with laughter. "I never look back," says Diane, "because I don't have time to do that. Michael has done a lot of nice things for a lot of people that needed it. I didn't realize before how much I learned from Michael that has helped me make certain decisions."

Out of the frying pan; into the fire. Within a year of Michael's divorce from Diane, he rebounded. He met Afifeh, a young woman who was a translator in Faye Awada's office on Warren Avenue in Dearborn. Michael was impressed by her capacity to help others.

"I found out she was related to me. She invited me to dinner with her mother. In 1990, I married Afifeh." It was an ill-advised marriage that ended seven and a half years later. "Thank God, I have two sons as a result of it, but I have had to pay a very heavy price. She does not want a life. Her sole purpose is to make my life miserable. They have joint legal custody of the boys, but she has custody because of their ages."

They lived on Fairmont. One day, Michael's good friend, Al Turfe, called him. "There's a ranch house in a subdivision that I think you might like to look at, if you are interested in a ranch-style house."

When Michael drove by the house, the FOR SALE sign had a SOLD sign attached to it. The house, as it turned out, was owned by Dr. Pickard, a former classmate of Michael's…all the way back to high school. The person who purchased the house could not come up with the mortgage, so Michael bought the house. On the last day of 1993, Michael moved into that house, and Al Turfe moved into Michael's house on Fairmont. "He has excellent taste," says Al. "I didn't have to lift a finger."

In February 1997, Michael and family were in Florida. He had gone to the bus stop to pick the boys up from school, and they were walking back to their oceanfront condo in Fort Lauderdale.

"Suddenly I collapsed," Michael tells. "It's a fortunate thing that I hit the pavement, because my heart had stopped and when I hit the pavement, the impact started my heart again. The boys were milling around, crying, 'My daddy's dead. My daddy's dead.' Some of the people in the condo office called for an ambulance. I was taken to the Cleveland Clinic, which has a branch clinic just two miles away from there. I stayed there than night.

Michael Berry & Frank Kelley, 2001

"The next day, the doctors had diagnosed the problem – heart failure, three arteries blocked. They said they wanted to operate, but I insisted on being returned to Michigan to see my own doctors at Beaumont Hospital. I had been under the care of Dr. O'Neill, the head of cardiology.

"I flew back to Detroit. One of my doctor friends, Dr. Ali Makki, from Michigan had flown to Fort Lauderdale to accompany me back to Michigan. We went directly to Beaumont. Dr. William B. O'Neill came in and said, 'We're going to have to perform open heart surgery. Here's a list of all the surgeons. Select the one you want.'

"I said, 'Doctor, I have no experience in this. I don't know who to choose.'

"He said, 'It's not ethical for me to make a choice for you; however, this man – Dr. Bassett – operated on my father.'

"So I said, 'If this man was good enough for your father, he's good enough for me.' They rushed me to the operating room. I had no chance to talk to my family. They put in three bypasses and one valve.

"Dr. O'Neill was the very first cardiologist to install a valve without performing open heart surgery. That procedure was introduced in 2005. I'm still under his care. Frank Kelley introduced him to me. They're both Irish – Kelley and O'Neill. Dr. O'Neill is a cardiologist and great humanitarian, and Frank Kelley is a remarkable human being who was the youngest attorney general in the nation when he was first elected to that post. By the time he was ready to retire, he had become the oldest attorney general in office. I am proud to say he is my friend."

Chapter 16

Timothy & Brendan Berry

L to R: Timothy, Michael, Brendan Berry

Timothy

Shortly after Michael received his son Timothy into the world, someone called Russ Gibb and gave him the good news. He called Michael to congratulate him and couldn't resist a little ribbing. "At your age, Mike...tell me, how did you do it?" [Michael was 71.]

"Hummos," teased Michael. "If you eat a lot of it, you'll have the same success."

The next day, he sent an order of hummos to Russ. That was Michael's sense of humor: Arabic Viagra.

However, Timothy was born August 14, 1991. Most notable about him is the striking physical resemblance he bears to his father. Other than patience, excellence in the sciences, and a desire to become a doctor, the resemblance fades. "I never knew my father wanted to be a doctor," he says.

At a very young age, Timothy observed his father practice law in his office on Warren Avenue in Dearborn. "My brother and I used to go there and watch him and our sister Laura, who was in the same office. I decided I wanted to become a doctor, because lawyers don't make as much money as they used to."

Although he would like to play basketball and go to Michigan State University, Timothy readily admits that "the job comes first." Work before play has been the family mantra. "Homework comes first. It's priority one. My Dad tries to do the best for us, encouraging us to always do better, because that will prepare us for college."

Timothy considers the age difference between Michael and the fathers of Timothy's friends insignificant, but it has drawn a few jokes from schoolmates, but no serious teasing. "They say things like, your dad is older than my grandpa."

Joking around and playing pranks go with the territory of being one of Michael Berry's offspring. "One day when we were at Kroger's, I told my Dad I wanted some gum, and he said okay. He doesn't like sour things. I got some sour gum, and just as he was at the cashier, I offered him a piece. He made a face when he started to chew it, and the cashier thought it was funny."

Timothy took action when his father's heart stopped a few years ago. "That was a bad day, a real bad day. He was walking Brendan and me home from school, and his heart just stopped. I called the ambulance. That was a rough time. He went to Beaumont Hospital. I was with my mom. They were divorced at the time, so I didn't know what was going on until I got to the hospital and saw him. I thought he would make it, and he did."

When Timothy has kids of his own someday, he will proudly share memories of his father's achievements. "He was a lawyer for more than 50 years. The International Terminal was named after him, the career center, and the Henry Ford Community College Amphitheater. He also gave a lot to Davenport University. At my old school – the American Islamic Academy on Schaefer – they named the gym after him."

Most of all, Timothy will remember that his father, Michael Berry, was a great father.

Brendan

While Brendan Berry, born September 8, 1993, bears less physical resemblance to his father, he makes up for it by sharing many of the same personality traits.

The first things that come to mind about his father are that he's a "really nice guy, smart, and straightforward. He does things the right way. I know that, because he tells us to get things done right. He's really strict. He wants us to do things the right way, because that's how he did them."

That applies to schoolwork. "I can't put off my homework until later. I have to do it first and get it out of the way, before I can do anything else. If I don't get a good grade, Dad will make me do some extra credit work to prove that I can do it. That's fair."

Brendan's favorite subject is English; he likes to write. "I want to be a lawyer and a politician, practicing either criminal law or municipal law. I would rather do something good than think about how much money I would make."

His leaning toward following in his father's footsteps comes as no surprise to anyone who has observed the two of them together. They are quite alike. "I like to argue," says Brendan. "I win sometimes when I argue with my dad, but he wins most of the time, because he's right."

Another similarity between Brendan and his father is his love of cars. "I love cars! He taught me about them. My favorite car is the Mercedes S600 or the Mercedes sports car, the SLR. It costs half a million dollars!" A conversation with Brendan and a complete stranger often starts with "What kind of car do you drive?"

Brendan enjoys his father's sense of humor, and the two of them are often seen ribbing each other. "When I was little, he used to tell little made-up stories about the jungle. He would change his voice to sound like a hyena or some other animal. He's a good storyteller."

When Brendan has children of his own some day, he will have many memories to share with them, but for certain, he will tell them that his father was a "really good guy, very smart, and he accomplished a lot."

Chapter 17

Michael & Cindy Berry, Wedding Day, April 14, 2007 (Photo by Hisham Beydoun)

Michael & Cindy

"The first time I met Michael Berry, I thought he was a stuffy lawyer," says Cindy Hanes, who now sports a diamond engagement ring – and a wedding band – to that same lawyer. Years and circumstances have a way of changing one's perspective. To see how that change evolved in Cindy, we'll take a look at who she is, where she came from, and how she came to know the real Michael Berry.

Cindy was born and raised in Detroit in the Michigan/Livernois area. Her father was in plant security at Ford Motor Company, and her mother was a stay-at-home mom for a long time, and then she became a teacher's aide at the elementary school where Cindy and her four brothers and sister attended.

Cindy, the second eldest, graduated from Chadsey High School and, as young girls often desire, she wanted to leave home.

"I wanted to teach the mentally retarded. One of the reasons for that choice was when I was a kid I babysat for a woman who had four kids. The youngest boy was a change-of-life baby, and he had Downs Syndrome. I didn't get paid a lot – I was lucky to get a dollar, but I used to play with this boy a lot. I would work with him to get him to stand up. One day the mother came home and he was standing up, so proud of himself. His mother cried. That's when I knew I wanted to teach kids like that."

When she enrolled in Michigan State University, her intent was to teach the mentally challenged. "But as graduation approached, my father was so sick with cancer, I didn't pay much attention to graduation. In March 1976, I received my diploma in the mail. I couldn't attend graduation, because my father was sick and my mother did not drive. I had no way to get there. It really wasn't that important to me; at least, I received my diploma before my father died in April. I was the only one of the kids to get a college degree."

After her father died, her mother underwent a hysterectomy, which in those days required a longer period of recuperation. "Both of my parents had been involved in Democratic politics, and Mom had worked periodically in Congressman Dingell's office. I used to pass out campaign literature when I was 10 years old.

"That summer – 1976 – Congressman Dingell's office called to see if my Mom wanted to work for July and August. She explained that she had just had surgery, and the person then asked if she knew anyone else. The congressman wanted someone who was Polish, because at that time, it was important for his constituents.

"My mother suggested that I work there for the summer. I figured for a summer job that would work out perfectly. I left 23 years later...to the day!"

After first meeting Michael Berry and determining that he was a "stuffy lawyer," Cindy had an occasion in 1979 to serve on the planning committee for a banquet honoring Michael. "I didn't really know Mike, but Dottie Engle, Congressman Dingell's secretary, put me on the committee. Bette Misuraca and Tom Wickle from the county were on the committee, and Marilyn Knight was a volunteer. For me, it was just another event to plan. I used to plan the district fundraisers for Congressman Dingell."

Cindy was 25 and impressionable, and that night at the banquet, with so many people honoring Michael Berry for his achievements, she was impressed. "I figured there must be something special about him, but he was married at the time, so I thought nothing else about him. After that banquet, Mike threw a little thank-you party for those of us on the planning committee. That's when he gave Dottie a piece of luggage because, as he said, 'I am tired of seeing that old ratty bag you've been carrying around.' That old ratty bag was one I made. I would get out my sewing machine and whip up quilted bags. Everybody loved them, and they were quite the rage back then."

Years passed. In 1998, after Michael's divorce from Afifeh, he called Congressman Dingell's office to set up an appointment with him. Cindy answered the phone. "When he came into the office, I greeted him and talked to him. Dottie had passed away, so I was the only staff person that he knew. After his meeting, he left the office, but he called later and asked if I would go to lunch with him. I thought maybe he wanted to discuss an immigration case. He didn't do immigration work and occasionally our office got cases like that. I thought it would be a business lunch, nothing more. In fact, I did not think at all that it was personal. Not at all."

Cindy was 44 at the time. Before she went to lunch the next day with Michael, a young girl, Nicole, who worked in the office, said, "He's interested in you, Cindy."

"Oh, he is not!" Cindy scoffed. "I've known him for years."

The fact is a 22-year-old girl, half Cindy's age, saw something she didn't see.

Michael and Cindy went to Guliano's in Melvindale. "It had nothing to do with business. It was just a nice friendly lunch," she recalls. "Then, when I got out of the car back at work, he shook my hand. I thought, 'OK.' I wasn't expecting that. Now, every once in a while when I want to harass him, I'll shake his hand."

Michael called her the next day and said he had a campaign check for the congressman, but he wanted to give it to her personally to make sure Mr. Dingell got it. So they went to lunch at the Dearborn Inn. "I realized then that he was interested, because he said, 'How about if we go to dinner and you pick the restaurant?' A couple of weeks later – after the election, which kept me busy 24/7, I called Mike. I knew he liked Italian food, so I picked Fonte de Amour in Livonia. I had no idea what Fonte de Amour meant [Source of Love]; I chose it because it was an Italian restaurant!

"We agreed to meet there for dinner. It was cold, but I remember leaving my coat in the car. Also, I always wore crappy shoes for driving, and then I would switch into my good shoes when I arrived at my destination.

"Well, I forgot to change my shoes. I never should have told him, because he wouldn't have known the difference. He made a joke out of it, and told everyone about my shoes. I was going to excuse myself, go to the restroom, and then go to the car and switch shoes. Then I realized that no one would have seen my shoes under the table, and Mike was not looking at my feet!"

They had a nice dinner. When it was time to leave, Michael asked Cindy if she would like to see his house. She said yes, and there has been no turning back. They have been together ever since.

"I love Mike because he's a very kind and giving person. He will do more for someone else than he will do for himself. I told him that years earlier when we met, it wasn't meant to be; it was meant to be now. The age difference does not matter at all; Mike is so young at heart."

Although Michael officially retired in 2000, he still remains active, does pro bono work, and gives free advice to a lot of Americans and Arab Americans. "I'm like an old fire horse. I hear the gong, and I start..." he says.

Michael has more free time, but occasionally his lingering public life interferes with his private life. "There are times when he commits himself," says Cindy, "and I'll say, 'Why do you want to be with those people? They take advantage of you and don't appreciate you.' He'll agree, but then say, 'I like to accomplish things for others.' He's been doing it so many years, he can't stop."

Horsepower

Take most people – they're crazy about cars. I'd rather have a goddamn horse. A horse is at least human, for God's sake.

J. D. Salinger
American Author
1919 -

Chapter 18

The Classics

Michael Berry's love of the automobile might very well be genetic. After all, his father was a great fan of the cars that rolled off the assembly line at Ford, and his brother, Henry, who was four years older than Michael, was equally enamored. It is therefore not much of a stretch that the bug would eventually bite Michael.

In the late 1950s and early 1960s, he took that love to new heights, investing in his first luxury classic, a 1936 Rolls Royce Phantom III four-door sedan, reputedly owned by Sir Laurence Olivier. Michael used to joke about Sir Laurence Olivier making love to Janet Leigh in the back seat. "I joked about that on more than one occasion."

Michael had the car repainted dark blue with black fenders and a silver top. The car's V-12 engine, a forerunner of the spitfire engines developed during World War II, made it unusual. Another unusual feature was its right-hand open compartment for the chauffeur.

"You had to put a canvas over the open compartment when you weren't driving it or when it rained," Michael explains. It was a rare sight in this country to see someone drive on the "wrong" side of the car. "We used it for parties and various shows, such as at an event at Greenfield Village."

That was Michael's first classic car. He then became a member of the Rolls Royce owners club that led to his purchase of a number of other cars.

He bought several Rolls Royces, including 1925 Silver Ghost, a Roadster. It was the beginning of a lifelong love affair with elegant automobiles and fast race cars. He attended classic car shows and, as a result, came to know many of the dealers. He also became familiar with Hemmings and other classic car publications that opened the doors to friendships and fast cars.

1930 Hispano-Suiza

1927 Hispano-Suiza

One Englishman in New York sold Michael several cars, and another dealer, Tom Barrett in Arizona, has sold Michael eight or nine cars over the years. The story of one of those cars bears repeating. One day in the 1960s, Michael saw a White Horse Scotch ad in a magazine that featured a gorgeous, gleaming automobile set in sharp contrast to a barren desert. At the bottom of the ad, it read: Through the courtesy of Tom Barrett, Scottsdale, Arizona.

Michael called Mr. Barrett and asked him about the car. He also wanted to know if it was for sale.

The car, a 1927 Hispano-Suiza Phaeton, was a hand-built luxury car, which, at the turn of the last century, earned a reputation similar to that of the Rolls Royce in England. A Swiss engineer had designed the Hispano-Suiza vehicles for King Alfonso XIII of Spain, but not this particular car, Mr. Barrett explained. He told Michael he had just brought it in from South Africa, and yes, it was available for purchase. The vehicle required total restoration.

The two men proceeded to negotiate a price over the telephone and finally settled on $11,000. Upon receipt of proper remittance, Mr. Barrett shipped the car to Michael in Detroit. Michael bought the car sight unseen.

The Hispano-Suiza was, according to Michael, probably the best-engineered car of its day. It was also the easiest car to maneuver and drive. "The Swiss engineer was brilliant. He built an engine that today they are just starting to match. In 1972, General Motors advertised the new Buick with something new under the sun - an all aluminum engine with steel sleeve inserts, six cylinders, and overhead cam. So, this car in 1927 and its predecessors had all aluminum engines, six cylinders, and overhead cams. A really clean engine compartment, too.

"Tom shipped the car, and I received word that it would arrive in a couple of hours and where would I like to take delivery," recalls Michael. "I gave them directions to my mother's house. So I go over to her house to wait.

"My mother asked, 'Aren't you working today?' and I told her I was, but that I had a car coming. Well, when they pulled up with the car, it looked like a wreck; it was an old unrestored car.

"My mother said, 'I don't want no junk in my garage.'

"This car is not junk, Mother," Michael asserted. "I paid $11,000 for it."

'I thought your father was crazy,' she remarked, shaking her head in dismay, 'but you are crazier still.'

A couple of weeks later, Michael received a call from Milwaukee. A brewery owner there had seen the same ad and located Michael through Tom Barrett.

"I understand that you bought a car from Tom Barrett," the man said. "Do you mind if my wife and I come down and take a look at it?"

"No, not at all," said Michael.

"My wife is president of a carburetor company in Detroit," the man continued, "and she has to come to a board meeting. We'd like to stop by."

Little did Michael realize that he was trying to set him up. So they came and looked at the car.

"I'll tell you what," the man said. "I'll pay you what you paid Tom Barrett for this car."

"I didn't buy it to sell it," said Michael. He intended to restore the Hispano-Suiza.

"I'll pay all the expenses," the man offered.

"It's not for sale," Michael asserted.

Two weeks later, Michael received a telephone call. "We're coming to Detroit. Do you mind if my wife and I take another look at the car?"

"No, not at all."

"I'll tell you what," the man offered, "I'll give you $15,000 for the car just the way it is."

"It's not for sale," Michael said.

Michael wondered why this man was so interested in this particular car. He called Michael a month later and gave him an ultimatum...$16,000...an offer that was good for 10 days.

In the meantime, Michael checked on the man and found that he was president of a large brewery in Milwaukee. He had been a race car driver, who suffered injuries from a crash and walked with a limp.

The 10 days passed. The prospective buyer called, "I gave you 10 days. Today's the last day."

"Forget it. I'm not interested in selling," Michael replied.

That did not deter the man. He said he would be coming to Detroit and wanted to sit down and talk to Michael and look at the car again.

All that interest started spinning Michael's wheels, wondering what someone might have put in the car before it left South Africa - perhaps diamonds or drugs. Michael searched the car and found nothing suspicious.

When the man arrived, he donned a pair of overalls that he brought with him and went under the car. "I guess it's still the original," he said.

"Yes, it is," Michael acknowledged.

"I'll tell you what. This is my last offer. I'll give you $25,000 for it."

"Okay," Michael said. He accepted and the man gave him a check. He went to see his mother.

"Well, a man just bought that car," Michael told her, "and he will be taking it out of your garage."

His mother asked, "What did you sell it for?" fully expecting a different answer than the one Michael would give her.

"I sold it for $25,000."

"That man is crazier than you and your father!" she concluded.

Mariam's opinion did not keep Michael from collecting classics. He purchased a 1930 Issota-Fraschini Roadster Model Tipo 8-A that was the most expensive car in its day. Unlike the Hispano, Michael thought the Issota drove "like a truck."

1930 Isotta-Fraschini Roadster

He owned a Mercedes that once belonged to actor Edward G. Robinson, a Rolls Royce convertible that Tony Curtis owned at one time, and a Rolls Royce Phantom II convertible that formerly belonged to the King of Norway.

He then turned his attention to sports cars, and over the years owned four Thunderbirds, several Corvettes, Austin Healys, Alpha Romeos, and a lovely French car, the Delahaye, although it was not a sports car. The six-cylinder car was beautifully designed car by Chapron.

His next purchase was an Osca, which is an abbreviation for Organization Society for the Construction of Automobiles by the Maserati brothers. The little car, with a 1600-cc engine and double overhead cam, was really built as a race car by the Maseratis. They could not use their name on it, because they had sold their company to Fiat and were barred from using the name Maserati, a famous name in the racing world and in the manufacture of sports cars.

One day, Michael saw an ad for a red Ferrari, a v-12, 6-carburetor, trans-axle, 4.9-litre race machine that had been used in the La Mans 24-hour race, an unbelievable piece of machinery. He did not know that it had won that famous race. He flew to Boston with Henry and his neighbor, John Bohas, both mechanics, to check out the car.

1940 Rolls Royce 2025; formerly owned by Actor Tony Curtis

They soon realized that the car would require extensive restoration and engine work, but all the parts were there, so Michael bought it for $2,200. He had it shipped to Detroit, along with 22 wheels and other parts.

"On occasions, I would take it out and cruise up and down Telegraph Road," he reminisced. "I had a lot of fun with that car, but I did not realize its value. Vivian would always complain that it would kill me."

The Ferrari would eventually earn the title of Michael's favorite car, most likely because it was the most valuable car he has ever owned. The story about that gets better. Read on.

When he learned from the Luigi Chinneti Company in New York that it would cost $11,000 to rebuild the engine, Michael decided to sell the Ferrari, which he did by phone to a man in Ithaca, New York, who bought the car sight unseen for $2,200. That was a happy day for Vivian.

"I never bought cars with the intention of reselling them," says Michael. "My biggest mistake was not building a garage big enough to

Rolls Royce Phantom II; formerly owned by the King of Norway

store these cars and their parts.

"I sold the wheels separately for $20 or $30 and gave some of them away just to get rid of them." This was not the end of the Ferrari story.

"About a year later, I saw an ad in Hemmings listing the car as part of an estate after the gentleman died," Michael says. "Apparently he had had the engine restored but not the whole vehicle. Someone purchased the car at the estate auction for $17,000."

Michael's follow-up on this Ferrari revealed that it was purchased by the White Brothers of Philadelphia, who restored the vehicle, and sold it to an Italian count for $125,000! In the 1980s, when Mr. Ferrari passed away, all 12-cylinder cars made before his demise became exceptionally hot commodities. Because there were only three that were originally built for the LeMans race, and two of them were destroyed; the one Michael had owned was the only remaining one of its kind.

"They put a value of $2.3 million on this car," Michael says. "The car had been totally restored. I don't know who would have been crazy enough to buy it at that price, unless it was for a museum or by the factory itself."

Buying and selling so many cars eventually puts a pinch on storage

Red Ferrari, Michael Berry's favorite car

space, and whenever that happened, Michael would sell one or two of his cars.

Once, he had three cars for sale, including a 1979 Mercedes 540K convertible, which was worth $54,000 at the time. He received a call from a man in Washington State who wanted the Mercedes, so Michael sold it to him on a Sunday and said he would wire the money to Michael the next day. Michael then received a call from actor Steve McQueen, who wanted to buy it for his wife, Ali McGraw.

"Steve was a heck of a nice guy to talk to, so easy-going. A wonderful person," Michael remembers. He told Steve that he had already sold the car.

"Have you signed the title yet?" Steve asked.

"No," Michael replied.

"Have you got the deposit?" Steve further pressed.

"No."

"Well, you have a right to sell it," Steve offered.

"Steve, you wouldn't want me to do that to you," Michael said. "I gave this man my word."

"I'll give you $5,000 more," Steve said.

"I can't do that," Michael responded. "I appreciate the offer, but if you want to come to Detroit, I've got a number of cars, and you can take your pick of any of them."

Michael had as good a European collection as most people had among the top collectors. Steve promised to come to Detroit. Unfortunately, within four or five months, he was diagnosed with cancer and went to Mexico for treatment. He died some time later.

"I never got to meet him in person or sell him a car, but I found him to be an extremely interesting conversationalist."

Over the years, Michael owned other cars, including some that are not as commonly known as others are. These vehicles were stored in various garages all over the city. The little Italian sports car, Siata, he liked so much, he bought a pair of them, one with the original engine and the other with a Chevy V-8 engine. Another was a Ferrari 250-GT convertible with a Scaglietti body, a California model with a long wheelbase.

Age has not diminished Michael's interest in great cars. He still goes to auctions now and then, and if he sees a car he likes, he buys it.

Chapter 19

Thoroughbreds

Some time in the late 1960s, Michael's youngest brother, Frankie, who had a very outgoing personality, became involved with horses. One day, he enticed Michael to join him at the horse auction. "Come on, I'll show you around," he said.

Until that time, Michael had paid attention to horses only once in Florida when he and Vivian went to a race track, just to watch the horses, not to bet on them.

"Now I have a problem with auctions," Michael admits. "I love to go to auctions, car auctions especially, and I have been to many and have purchased cars at them, so I went to the horse auction with Frankie way out on the east side.

"I saw one young filly. Then I got into a bidding contest with someone I later learned was a member of the Mafia, or so I was told. He wanted the same filly that I wanted. She was gorgeous, a huge beauty. Already named Scoundrel Lady, she was by the Scoundrel, who finished second or third in the Kentucky Derby.

"Anyway, I didn't have anyone check her or the colt. I bought the colt and then got into a bidding war over the filly. She went for the highest price at the auction; I paid twice for her what I paid for El Amir, the colt."

As it turned out, Scoundrel Lady couldn't run her way out of a paper bag. Michael bred her and got a colt out of her, who was also afraid of his own shadow. He eventually sold Scoundrel Lady.

El Amir, on the other hand, did well and won quite a few races. They were claiming races, however, which meant that someone – anyone – could put up anywhere from $2,500 to $25,000 to claim a horse at the track, depending on the value of the race.

"Any person who has a horse at that track can put up the amount of money required and if no one else claims him, it's that person's horse,"

Sten, thoroughbred champion

Michael explains. "Once the gates are open and the horse runs, whoever has the claim owns the horse. If the horse dies on the track, that person still has to put up the claim money."

Sten

Over the years, Michael claimed a few and lost a few horses, all thoroughbreds. In 1978 when Michael attended a horse auction in Kentucky, he bought a well-bred two-year-old by the name of Sten. He had been sent back from New York, because he didn't seem to be able to run.

"I looked at Sten's pedigree and was amazed at what a nice one he had," recalls Michael. "As I was looking over the pedigree and Sten, a trainer I knew in Florida named Tony Everrard, approached. I said, 'Tony, look at this horse for me.' He said he was coming to look at the same horse, but if I could buy him, I should do so.

"Tony didn't know anything about Sten's running problem. The horse came up very late in the sale, around 10 or 11 p.m. on a bitter cold November night. There was just one other person at the end that was bidding. He bid $9,500 for Sten, and the bidding increments were by the hundreds. I finally bid $9,800 for him, and the other party dropped out,

```
                         THE  CHINA RUN
    AQUEDUCT, NEW YORK  PURSE  $22,000  APRIL 6,1979
    MICHAEL BERRY OWNER      STEN       CASH ASMUSSEN UP
    R.T. DeSTASIO TRAINER               1 1/8 MILES TIME 1:53:3
          ROYAL FLAVOUR 2nd       QUIET CROSSING 3rd
```

Sten, a winning thoroughbred

and I got the horse. Tony took the horse to Ocala.

"Two weeks later, Tony called. 'Mike, this horse can't run. We could probably sell him as a stallion.' I asked what he would bring as a stallion, and Tony said maybe $20,000 to $25,000 or we could geld him and see if he could run.

"I told Tony I would think about the options and call him later.

Finally I called back and told him, 'Geld him. Let's take a try.' So they had him gelded.

"About a month later, I received a telephone call from Tony. 'We've got a stakes horse on our hands!' Of course, I was thrilled. 'I'll finish up his training,' Tony said, 'then where do you want me to send him?' I told him I didn't know anyone in particular."

Tony suggested Michael send the horse to New York to a trainer he felt was trustworthy – Richard (Dick) DeStasio. Michael made the arrangements and shipped Sten to Dick. The horse won a few races and then Dick put him in a stakes race, a graded stakes race. In that stakes race was a horse ranked the best grass horse in the country at that time - John Henry. Also in that race was the European champion, Lyphard's Wish, and Sten. He came from behind and won the race, and then went on to win a few more races.

"We entered him in the Arlington Million. He was training in Saratoga Springs, New York. We had great hopes for him to win that race. Whenever I went to see him, I took along Mary Jane candies, which Sten loved. When he would see me coming, he would stick his head out of the stall and wait until I peeled the wrappers off the Mary Janes. If I didn't give him any, he would nudge me in my jacket to get them.

"Sten was doing very well in training. He won the Bowling Green Handicap, defeating John Henry and Lyphard's Wish and several others, while in training for the Arlington race.

"The entry fee for the Arlington Million was approximately $75,000. The first payment was $20,000, a non-refundable deposit that assures your horse a place in the race.

"One day, as Sten was coming off the training track, a garbage truck backfired. Sten reared up and came down hard on his front legs and injured one of them. My trainer's vet said we could do one of two things: keep him out of working out or operate and remove the splint. He had popped a splint. I asked the trainer what he suggested, and he said we would not be able to make the race unless we operated."

Michael gave the nod for surgery on Sten, but it turned out to be an unfortunate decision, because the surgeon did not do a good job. He left a rough edge, which rubbed against the suspensary. Sten was never able to run again. The incident cost Michael $20,000, but he came away with a jacket, which he refers to as his $20,000 jacket.

Silver Supreme

Silver Supreme

Some time later, Michael and his second wife, Diane, were at an auction in Kentucky. Unbeknownst to Michael, she was bidding on a colt. Michael turned around. "What the hell are you doing?" he asked her. By then, the bidding was up to $12,000.

"He's so beautiful," she said. Michael took over the bidding and bought the horse for $15,000. The most Michael ever paid for a horse was about $50,000. Today, the price tag is in the millions for a pedigreed thoroughbred.

Michael's trainer, Dick, said that Silver Supreme would never make it to the races. Considering how well bred the horse was, Michael wondered why Dick said something like that. "Well he won't be the kind of horse you're looking for," Dick replied. "He has long pasterns."

Several other people in New York and elsewhere told Michael the same thing, so Michael entered him in the sale, and no one bid more than $8,000, so as the auctioneer was yelling, "Going once, going..." Michael bid $9,000 and bought his own horse back.

"It was the smartest thing I ever did. We got him running. He

```
BELMONT PARK,N.Y.    PURSE  $21,000        JULY 23,1981
MICHAEL BERRY OWNER  SILVER SUPREME        CASH ASMUSSEN UP
R.T.DeSTASIO TRAINER                       1 MILE TIME 1:36
         SHAHNAMEH 2nd        PIROUETTE 3rd
```

Silver Supreme, another winner

turned out to be a fabulous distance horse, a classic. I named him Silver Supreme. A man named Joe bought an interest in him after he won his first two regular races. He paid $125,000 for a quarter interest in Silver Supreme.

"Then he ran in the Yankee Handicap in Massachusetts. I wasn't there, but Joe was there. Silver Supreme broke out just before the race and fortunately, he won that race.

A few months later, the Massachusetts Handicap, which is the biggest race in that state, came up and the top horses were there from all over the country. Silver Supreme was entered, and Michael flew up to Boston.

The race was underway, and Silver Supreme was running so far back, Michael started to leave. "Hey, he's running now," everyone started yelling. "Come back!"

Silver Supreme won that race by two lengths. He was an awesome horse.

1980 was a great year for Silver Supreme; he was winning some big races. He won the Brooklyn Handicap, a classic, grade one race, which runs a mile-and-a-half in length. That race is now a Grade 2. A grade one is the highest type of achievement a horse can get in racing.

Silver Supreme should have won the Jockey Cup Gold Cup, but took second in this grade one race. "It was a terrible race in that three horses broke down and Silver Supreme had to go around them or jump over them," Michael explains. "Timely Writer broke his leg and went down. The horse directly behind him ran into him and went down. And the horse behind him collided and went down. Cordero was riding Silver Supreme, and he steered him to the extreme right of the horse to almost the fence and came back. In the meantime, another horse shot ahead of us and won the race, leaving us in second place. We had had to make up a lot of ground. Had it not been for the accident, we would have won."

After Silver Supreme won the grade one race, Michael received a call from someone he had met in New York, a fine gentleman by the name of Bill Garbarini. He was a close friend and partner on some other horses with a man by the name of Michael Martin, who with his father owned a bank and trust company in Philadelphia. Michael Martin's father was a member of the Jockey Club, a very prestigious organization nationwide.

Bill Garbarini asked Michael if he would be interested in selling a third of Silver Supreme.

"Make me an offer," said Michael.

"How can I get to see you?" asked Bill.

"I'm here in Florida. Do you want to come down? We can talk," Michael offered.

They met at the Rain Dancer, a steak house on Commercial Street

The Meadowlands
The Violet Stake
Won by Rash But Royal
Michael Berry
September, 1, 1983

in Pompano Beach. Bill offered Michael one million dollars for a third of the horse. Michael accepted.

After that, Silver Supreme ran a couple of times, but did not win. By then, he was five years old, so Michael and the others decided to send him to a farm in northern New York near Saratoga. Bill owned the farm with someone else. They put Silver Supreme up for stud, and the first couple of horses that came from him did nothing.

"They were not like their father. Bill really was interested in buying a third of the horse, but I said no. So they in turn found buyers from Argentina. I said, go ahead and sell him, which they did for $200,000. That was the last I heard of Silver Supreme."

Had Silver Supreme come on the scene a bit earlier, he would have been a strong contender for the Kentucky Derby. That track is a mile and a quarter, and Silver Supreme ate up the Belmont track, which is a quarter of a mile longer. The Derby would have been right up his alley.

Community
& Humanity

Dedicate some of your life to others.
Your dedication will not be a sacrifice.
It will be an exhilarating experience because it is an intense
effort applied toward a meaningful end.

Thomas Dooley, MD
Humanitarian
1927-1961

Chapter 20

Tallal Turfe has known Michael since he was knee-high. The two of them worked tirelessly to form, reform, and transform various organizations in the greater Detroit community, as well as in Dearborn.

"Our two families were probably the closest," Tallal recalls. "My dad, Alie Turfe, would take contributions for charity, and Mike would give him a blank check, signed, and would tell him to write the number he wanted. My dad would write one thousand, two thousand..." That's it, Michael would say, it's yours.

"He would take charity to help poor people; he had a lot of that in him. He was always there, even if he were to collect it for Bint Jbeil, Mike would be the first to donate, even though that's not his village. He's very, very cooperative and charitable. He donated to all the mosques, not just one."

Others echo that sentiment, like retired Wayne County Circuit Court Judge Charles Farmer. "One of my strongest impressions of Mike is that he is known to put his money and his heart where his mouth is. A lot of people talk, but they don't act. Mike acts. He is trustworthy, honest, and a good man. When he's your friend, you know it. We trust each other immensely."

Arab American & Jewish Friends

For years, Michael set the pace in service to the Arab American community and encouraged outreach to people of other communities and faiths. One such example was the founding in the late 1970s of the Arab American and Jewish Friends (AAJF) organization, for which Michael was one of the earliest proponents.

The purpose was to bring together all factions from both sides - Arab Christians, Arab Muslim, and Arab Jews. On the other side were orthodox Jews, reformed Jews, and conservative Jews. Despite early ups and downs, the organization remained relatively secret while the individual groups came to a better understanding of their respective cultures and beliefs. In more recent years, the organization has held annual dinners and scholarship-motivated essay contests for high school seniors.

Tallal and Michael worked to bring the AAJF into the Greater Detroit Interfaith Roundtable of the National Conference on Community and Justice, formerly the National Conference of Christian and Jews. Michael was instrumental in having the NCCJ bring Muslims and people of other faiths into the spectrum, so that all faiths would be represented. He was the first Muslim to serve on the NCCJ Board.

"That was Mike Berry working particularly with Lebanese who had immigrated to the United States," said Tallal. "He helped a number of them get jobs and become good citizens. He does this in the keen and structured way. It's almost like the LEAP method – he listens very well, asks questions, probes like a lawyer would. He digs and analyzes, but he does this not to turn off the people but to help make them understand their perspectives more clearly. So, for the Lebanese who came here, Mike would sit with them and help them understand American government. He did this quite well, and a number of people are grateful to him for doing so."

Michael did three things: he transformed communities of value for our Lebanese Americans by working with them and helping them assimilate into the mainstream. He reshaped the landscape, because even in a lot of organizations he was able to use the conventional method of organization and bring our people into the fold. He redefined the interior of our community, so now it has mushroomed from what Dearborn and Dearborn Heights were pre-1970s to now.

"Mike has played a very important and integral role in reshaping the landscape. He interfaces well with the leaders of all these organizations, as well, so he's brought them into the fold to work together. I think really that is what his knack has been."

Michael understands these people, Tallal asserts, including their shortcomings when they come here to adjust to the American way of life, but he's patient. "It's not a passive patience, but a pro-active patience. He's tolerant. He has a good ear for listening, and he listens. He reaches out...to me, to my younger brother.

"My father, in his last days, clasped Mike's, my brother's and my hands in his and said, 'I now turn my kids over to you.' We were all adults – this was in 1990 – but my father saw a sense of family and relationship, and he wanted a fatherly image for us, so Mike was there, just like a big brother."

United American Lebanese Association

In the 1980s, Michael worked with members of the Arab American community to form the United American Lebanese (UAL) Association. "At the height of the strife in Lebanon with clashes, war, and disaster there, we brought together the Druze, Protestants, Catholics, Sunnis, Shiites – people from every faction – keeping in mind that most of these people were immigrants from Lebanon, while Mike and I were born and raised in the United States. We gathered at the Hyatt Regency in Dearborn, and it turned out great. We had music, dancing, and speeches, and while the war was raging in Lebanon, we were getting along quite well.

"That's a testimony to Mike's ability to bring people together from diverse backgrounds and faiths. For a person of his stature to roll up his sleeves and dig in – and even receive abuse at times because people didn't understand at the moment but later realized he was right. It was only a matter of time. He was doing it for their own good, when he would give them advice, so they turned to respect him.

"The Islamic Center of America and the Islamic Institute of Knowledge look to Mike for his counsel and advice. These are the two major Islamic organizations from the Shiite perspective. Then there's the Lebanese Athletic Club that turns to him for counsel, and the Bint Jbeil Cultural Center.

ACCESS

Like every other Arab American, Ismael Ahmed, Executive Director of the Arab Community Center for Economic and Social Services, knew about Michael Berry before he knew Michael Berry. "He was an icon for many of us, a powerful force on the political scene in the county when we knew very little about county government. When Southeast Dearborn was threatened to become an industrial park, he was one of the early ones to challenge it. He was considered an attorney extraordinaire in this community who would pick up the battle of the little guys. That was the reputation he had. He also had the reputation of someone you would go to for advice on the big questions of the day. In my formative years, that's the Michael Berry I knew of; I didn't know him personally."

As Ahmed became an activist involved in the Arab American community in the 1970s, he began to run into Michael Berry. "He had a lot more experience than I had, and I didn't think anyone knew anymore than I knew, so we bumped heads on several things, but in the end I came more and more to see his long-term wisdom. I used to watch him hold court in different restaurants. Just about any time I would to go to a restaurant, there he was, meeting with somebody who was a leader in the mainstream. I realized that this was a person who systematically built relationships not only for himself but also for the community in a way that no one else was doing at the time."

Ahmed eventually sat down with Michael and talked about the concerns of the community and the work of ACCESS. They resolved whatever differences they had, and since then, Michael Berry has been not only a mentor in theory but also one in practice. "I routinely go to him for advice and intelligence and viewpoint. He has been very, very supportive of ACCESS and the creation of the National Arab American Museum; he's on the board of the museum. A room is named for him there, and there is a little exhibit about Michael in the 'Did You Know?' section.

"We have worked together on local and national politics. We don't always agree, but I always know that there's intelligence behind anything he does, and that he is always acting in the interest of what he believes the community needs.

"He is one of the people that I know is going to be consistent and engaged and usually on the mark, so although it's hard for us to get together often, I try always to stay in touch with him. His stamina, his will, and his sheer physical strength, given all he's been through, are quite amazing."

In 2005, ACCESS honored Sir Michael Berry [the title awarded by the Lebanese government in 1993] for his contributions to the community and to ACCESS. "Once a year we identify a couple of people that we believe are icons, the people who have a long, long history of giving and acting on the community's behalf."

One on one

Michael often encounters individuals that need advice or assistance in solving a problem, and he often put qualified people in jobs. He still finds

Actor Jamie Farr (l) with Michael Berry & Cindy Hanes, ACCESS Banquet, 2005

time to mentor young business entrepreneurs like Kamal "Kal" Turfah. "Look at the age difference between Michael Berry and me; I'm 29 and he's 86, yet he takes time to listen to my ideas and my problems and give me sound advice. For someone my age to have someone like him as my friend is really something. In this life, you've got to love what you do, and he loved his work and that's why he was so successful. He put his heart into his work, and it showed. He truly made a difference; he still does."

Michael found time to help someone like young Mike Guido, get his first job with Wayne County, cutting the grass along Hines Drive Parkway. [Mike Guido later became mayor of the city of Dearborn and served for 14 years as such; he recently died while this book was being written.]

"You had to have a sponsor in order to get one of these jobs," Mike Guido said. "He was Uncle Mike, and everyone wanted a job. He put me on the payroll, but I worked hard and never embarrassed him. I worked on that job for the summer of 1972 and again the next year.

"If you had lined up 200 kids that got summer jobs from Mike, he probably could not have pointed to me and said, 'That's Mike Guido.' He just knew that we were all Dearborn kids, and he took care of us. I think that's one of the things he will always be remembered for. He gave so many

people opportuni-
ties to work, to
prove themselves,
and to better
their lives. Almost
everyone who
worked on that
summer mow-
gang went on to
become profes-
sionals. We went
to college, but we
needed money to
go to school. He
recognized that."

Michael Berry
often counseled
young people,
giving them the
perspective of
his years of ex-
perience. Mona
Majzoub was one
who benefited by
his wisdom. "He

Michael Berry and Michael Guido

lived down the street from us on Fairmont. My father was a physician, a
very revered surgeon in the community. He and Mike Berry became best
friends. They really enjoyed each other's company. In their own separate
worlds, they were big shots, so there was a little one-upmanship going on,
but they respected each other.

"After I went to law school, my father suggested I talk to Mike to
get some ideas for my career. At the time I was working for a law firm in
Detroit. It was a great firm, and I was the only woman lawyer there.

"I went down the street and told him I was doing litigation work, but
I was interested in knowing if I should entertain any other ideas for my
career path, such as a judgeship – which was strictly my father's idea. Mike
said, 'Well, yes, but not for a long time. You've got to pay your dues. You
have to prove yourself. You can't just come out of law school and expect

to become a judge and be respected.'

"I thanked him and thought, 'well, I guess I'll come back and talk to you when I grow up.' Basically, that was what he was telling me.

"As it turned out, Mike was absolutely right, even though I didn't know what it meant at the time. I practiced law for 28 years. I did not have an ambition to become a judge, but it eventually evolved out of the blue. I was appointed a United States Magistrate Judge in the U.S. District Court in Detroit in January 2004. It is a big honor."

Sometimes Michael's generosity made people hesitant to call on him for advice or help.

"He always gave me good advice," says Gerald Nassar, whose family grew up in the same Highland Park neighborhood as the Berry family. "I always refrained from going to see him, because he never charged me. One time, he had an attorney do something for me, and that attorney sent me a bill. I sent a check to him."

Michael called Gerald, "What's this check for?"

"That's for the problem that the attorney took care of for me," Gerald explained.

"You don't have no bill," Michael said. "I'm tearing up your check."

That wasn't the only time he did that. Another incident involved a young woman, who had fallen into trouble. Gerald had turned to Michael for help with her situation. Michael got her out of jail on probation. She was married and had a young son.

After sending the girl out of the room, Michael asked Gerald, "Now what about the boy?"

Gerald explained that the boy was nice.

"Is the girl a good mother?" Michael asked.

"She's an excellent mother. She may be a tramp but before she goes out at night or does anything, that kid is taken care of. When she's not working in bars, she's taking care of the kid."

Michael told her how much it would cost to take care of her legal problems, but he refunded half of it back to her.

Education

A keen advocate of education, Michael Berry has contributed to the betterment of schools and the educational environment in his community. Sometimes, as in the next story, his support for education comes in a roundabout way.

Russ Gibb, retired video and media instructor at Dearborn High School, tells the story of an opportunity that arose for him to become involved in cable franchises. The Teleprompter Cable Company asked Russ if he knew any influential politicians. He told them the most influential politician he knew was Michael Berry, so they asked if Russ could get Michael to join them in this new venture.

"I called Mike and asked if he would like to come in with me, that I had a possibility of a deal with a cable company."

Michael's response was "You want me to be a rent-a-citizen?"

Russ quickly clarified the situation, that Michael's involvement would be a business deal, that the group would need lawyers.

Michael balked.

"We're trying to do something for the community," Russ insisted. Then he talked about public access, and finally education.

"What do you mean, 'education'?" Michael inquired.

"Well, there's a good chance we could do some things for the school system here, the community college, and the University of Michigan-Dearborn, and we would have programming," Russ explained.

Michael requested time to think about Russ's request. Not long afterward, Russ planned to go to New York to meet with people at this major cable company. He called Michael and asked if he would be willing to go with him. As it turned out, Michael was planning to take horses to New York, which he did by train. The cable company sent its limousine to pick him up.

"We were in the company's executive dining room overlooking Central Park. This was about 1972. The executive told Mike the company could pay him such-and-such, and Mike stopped him cold."

"Wait a minute," Michael interrupted. "I don't need your money, and I'm not a rent-a-citizen…"

The executive started to clarify his position, "We're planning to do something for education…"

"What?" Michael asked with renewed interest. "What would you do for education?"

The company executives then asked Michael what he would like to see come of the project.

"If you want me, here's what you have to do," Michael said. "You will have to guarantee that the Dearborn public schools will be deeply involved. Henry Ford Community College will be deeply involved, and the U of M-Dearborn will be deeply involved. If you can do good things for them, you'll have me on your side, but if it's just to benefit you or me, forget it. I'm not interested."

The cable company gave a million dollars to the schools, and that is why, Russ says, even today there is the Dearborn Cable Communications Fund that is not connected to the city or to a cable company. It is totally independent, run by citizens, and they give educational programs to Dearborn.

"It's been going on all these years," said Russ, "and in recognition, I wanted to name the studio at Dearborn High after Mike Berry, but he wouldn't have any of it. He just asked me to make sure the kids were taken care of."

Even as recently as two years ago, Russ asked Michael to let him name the studio after him. It's a two million dollar studio that brings in kids from other schools, not just Dearborn High. Michael still refuses. "But that is Mike Berry."

Chuck Shamey likes to tell another story that reveals Michael's determination to make the best education available to children in the community. "We went to get Mike's hair cut. A young teen-aged girl was working there, and she was telling us her story, her hard-luck story, her plight with school. Mike quizzed her while he was having his hair cut.

"When we were alone, he looked at me and said, 'We've got to see the superintendent. We've got to start changing things. These kids are falling through the cracks.' Mike is genuine. He loves children and wants the best for them."

Michael and Chuck served on the American Islamic Academy School Board for 14 months. "We formed a quick bond," said Chuck, former principal at Riverside Academy in Dearborn Heights. "Mike respects everybody but I think he respects that I worked my way through the system and ultimately became a school principal, which isn't an easy thing to do."

Michael Berry has made a significant contribution to Henry Ford Community College; for that, they named the amphitheater for him. For his substantial efforts on behalf of Dearborn Public Schools, the Michael Berry Career Center was named after him. The Center, located at Ann Arbor Trail and Outer Drive in Dearborn Heights, belongs to the Dearborn Public School system. He has given generously to Davenport University in Dearborn and serves as a Trustee Emeritus on that board.

Center for Arab-American Studies (CAAS)

When the University of Michigan/Dearborn decided to launch a Center for Arab American Studies, they turned to Michael Berry and Edward Deeb to serve on the founding committee. The founder and chairman of the Michigan Food & Beverage Association, and CEO of the Michigan Business & Professional Association and Eastern Market Merchants Association, Ed has known Michael for many years. "I first met Mike when he was chairman of the Wayne County Road Commission. I was involved with grocers, restaurants, supermarkets and the like, and we would often find ourselves at the same meetings, which involved transportation and road repairs."

Over the years, Michael and Ed, who share the Lebanese heritage, worked on different projects involving the Arab American community. Then one day in 2003, they received a call from Paul Wong, dean of the College of Arts, Sciences & Letters at the University of Michigan-Dearborn.

They met over breakfast at the Ritz, and Paul explained that he had just started the Center for Arab American Studies, the first academic center to focus on people from the Arab world who live in the United States. The center was founded on a cooperative spirit and work with other Michigan academic institutions, including the University of Michigan-Ann Arbor, University of Michigan-Flint, Eastern Michigan University, Wayne State University, and Henry Ford Community College.

The Center established four goals: to teach students, professionals, and the general public about Arab Americans; to form a hub for research around which interested scholars can investigate, present, and publish their work; to encourage a dialogue on critical policy issues among Arab American cultural, economic, religious, and social service organizations on the one hand, and policy makers, educators, and researchers on the other; and finally, to preserve the records and histories of the Arab American community.

"Paul explained that he was looking for two people – one prominent in the Arab Muslim community and the other prominent in the Arab Christian community – to bring everyone together," Ed recalls. "He asked Mike and me to co-chair this beautiful program. With our backgrounds and connections, we felt we could make things happen. To our chagrin, about eight months later, Paul announced that he was leaving to

L to R: Edward Deeb, Rabab Abdulhadi, first CAAS chair & Michael Berry, 2006

take a position at San Diego State University."

Since that time, the program has slowed down, but not for lack of enthusiasm on the part of Michael Berry and Ed Deeb. "We had some high ideals, but every time we started to talk about doing something, someone would throw a monkey wrench into it. Mike and I have met several times and discussed what needed to be done.

"I've come to know Mike over the years as a very well respected individual, who is well liked. You can sense the charisma he has by the people who have flocked to him all these years. I feel fortunate to be able to work with him on a very close basis."

"Michael Berry is the dean of our community," Al Turfe says. "He knows how to motivate people to get involved in education, politics, and social services. I think he will be remembered as the first and foremost person others sought for advise, leadership, and help...for his guidance and counseling...his wisdom. He's done a lot for this community. He's a bridge builder. He can bring people together, and he knows how to resolve problems."

William Clay Ford, Jr. & Michael Berry, 2005

"I think Michael Berry showed a lot of people the way in terms of how to become not just a successful lawyer but also a leader," Mona Majzoub adds. "He shows true leadership for the Arab American community. He did things that most people have not done. He successfully aligned himself strategically in a way that allowed him to accomplish great things. He was investigated backwards and forwards when he was with the Road Commission and nobody could find one dime out of place.

"The Road Commission was truly his baby. He just knew how to get things done. From the beginning, he understood power bases, resources, the importance of education, the importance of hard work. He could pull strings and get things done. The Arab community does not have many leaders like Mike Berry, and I do not know that they will ever have another one like him."

Chapter 21

Michael's desire to make a difference in the world could not be contained by a community or a state. Over the years, he followed his mother's early example to take up the cause of impoverished people in Lebanon, raising funds for the health care and well being of a population ravaged intermittently by the hardships of war.

His charity was issued without fanfare or expectation of anything in return for his generosity. This is the mark of a true humanitarian.

"Mike Berry is the one person I can positively say is a humanitarian," says Dr. Avery Jackson, who worked with Mike on the Wayne County Road Commission. "He has a heart of gold. It's the way he lives, the way he conducts his life and helps people without regard to race or religion, but if it happens to be a person of a particular nationality, so be it."

American Task Force for Lebanon

In 1979, Michael became one of the founders of the American Task Force for Lebanon, a Washington-based organization created to improve relations between Lebanon and the United States and to improve the status of Lebanese-Americans in this country.

The ATFL is a nonprofit organization comprised primarily of prominent and dedicated Americans of Lebanese heritage who share a common interest in Lebanon and the goals of the organization. The unifying goal is to work towards reestablishing a secure, stable, independent, and sovereign state with full control over all its territory.

Michael became active in the organization and was appointed to the executive committee, and today he serves on the executive board. He was the only Muslim Lebanese in the organization and today is the only Muslim Lebanese on the executive board, although there are two or three others on the general board.

In its mission to set policy for facilitating peace and reconstruction in Lebanon, Michael has had the opportunity to meet with Cardinal

Mooney of the New York Diocese. Shortly after that meeting, a special meeting was called with President George Herman Walker Bush. "The Cardinal set up the meeting and requested that a total of seven members of the ATFL be present – the most prominent members," Michael recalls. "The meeting was to be held in the Oval Office in the White House. I was honored to be selected as one of those seven members representing not just the United States but for all of North America.

"I went to Washington, met the president, and had my picture taken. We expressed our concern about what was happening in the Middle East. At the time, the United States had refused the right of Middle East Airlines to land in this country and had asked that no American airliner land in Lebanon. He listened to us and agreed in principle about what should be done. This was at the end of what we thought would be his first term in office. He promised that right after the election, he would take care of the matter. Unfortunately, Bush did not get re-elected. Bill Clinton won, and that was the end of that. We never went to see him."

In his service with this organization, Michael has worked alongside former New Hampshire Governor John Sununu, Dr. Michael DeBakey, former U. S. Senate Majority Leader George Mitchell, Casey Kasem, Cardinal John O'Connor, and former President Jimmy Carter.

Michael plays an important part in working toward a balanced policy with Lebanon, financial aid, and adequate housing crusades. Michael has been recognized many times for his effective leadership in promoting peace, harmony, and justice in the Middle East.

With civil war ravaging Lebanon, particularly South Lebanon, Michael Berry, Tallal Turfe, other Lebanese-American leaders, and Dr. Robert Simon, a Chicago physician, were deeply moved by the fact that three government-run hospitals in South Lebanon were slated to close, due to lack of operating funds. They set out to raise the needed aid, and succeeded in providing $1.6 million in medical supplies and equipment to save those hospitals in 1992.

"Mike's ingenuity, tactfulness, and diplomacy worked well to bring together 40 individuals, including his neighbor, Hamze Abbas, who took the shipment to Lebanon and saw to it that the distribution was fairly divided to each hospital. Each of those individuals contributed from $500 to $20,000, so we could send someone and ship the materials to Lebanon," Tallal relates. "That's what we did, and it was a huge success."

Whether it has been trying to secure a balanced foreign policy in the

Middle East or maintain a fair and level playing field for Arab Americans here in the United States, Michael Berry has carried the torch high. As a true ambassador, his advice and wise counsel has been sought by United States presidents and leaders of foreign countries.

Michael Berry's Service to Community & Humanity

PRESENT

American Arab Anti-Discrimination Committee
Advisory Board

American Task Force for Lebanon
Founding Member
Board of Directors
Executive Committee

Arab American & Chaldean Council
Advisory Board

Center for Arab-American Studies Committee
University of Michigan-Dearborn
Co-chairman

Arab American National Museum
Board of Trustees

Davenport University
Trustee Emeritus

Henry Ford Community College
Foundation Board of Trustees

Islamic Institute of Knowledge
Legal Advisor

NAACP
Life Member

PAST

American Arabic & Jewish Friends
Honorary Chairman

Children's Hospital, Detroit, Michigan
Board of Trustees

Dearborn United Community Services
Director

**Greater Detroit Round Table of National Conferences
of Christians, Jews & Muslims**
Board of Directors
Chairman & President

Keep Detroit Beautiful Committee
Member

March of Dimes
Board of Directors

Michigan Arthritis Association
Board of Trustees

St. Jude Children's Research Hospital
Board of Directors

Southeast Dearborn Civic Association
Honorary President

**Task Force for Ethnic & Racial
Discrimination in the Courts**
Appointed by the
Michigan Supreme Court G. Mennon Williams

United American Lebanese Association
First Co-Chairman

Wayne County Citizens Committee on Juvenile Delinquency
Member

World Lebanese Union - Michigan
Past President

Recognition
& Rewards

*Our heroes are those...who...act above and beyond the call
of duty and in so doing give definition to patriotism and elevate
all of us. America is the land of the free, because it is the
home of the brave.*

David Mahoney
American Author

Chapter 22

When Mike Berry was young, he was no different than a lot of us who were starting out, and Mike's philosophy was the same as my father's, that was, if other people had to walk a mile to do something, he would walk two. It was that way with all the people who started out in this country, whether you were Lebanese or Polish or Italian or Irish. You had those constraints. You were typecast at the beginning, and Mike certainly was a camel jockey, but he overcame that with his natural wit and industry and hard work.

I would have to say that Mike is as typical of the success-oriented Middle Easterner who was born here but his family came from overseas. There was such a fierce desire to succeed among those people. It's nothing new, but it certainly made America great. And I would certainly consider Mike to be one of the building blocks of our country.
—George Bashara

To know Mike Berry is to know our community, which is a very close knit one. When we accomplish things, we're proud of each other. I always knew about Mike when I was growing up. I knew about his great law firm, his great political background, his involvement in Michigan politics. What I was doing in the 1960s, Mike did in the 1930s. He is old enough to be my father, but he's my friend.

One of the things I admire about Mike is his service to the community and to our people. He always, always wants to help. That's what I love about him. I don't know if everyone loves the South End like I do, but I love it. I love Salina. I love to hear Mike's stories of growing up there in the 30s. **—Chuck Shamey**

People forget what Mike Berry did 20 years ago. They haven't been around here long enough. They don't really know the history of Mike Berry. They don't really remember when he was Wayne County Road Commissioner and all the Arabs he helped get into jobs.

Mike Berry stood up and said that he was an Arab at a time when Arabs were viewed as dogs. Today, if you stand up and say you're an Arab, you have different political groups behind you that are becoming a political force, but when he did that, the papers hounded him.

I firmly believe that Mike Berry has done more for this community than any Arab I can think of. He has stood up first and foremost for the community, more than anyone else has done. —**Brian Mosallam**

Michael Berry, my dear cousin, is the godfather of our family and of our community. Whenever someone reaches out to Mike for any type of help or assistance, he has always been there for them. If it were in his power to do so, he would help anyone that needed his assistance. I appreciate the guidance and wisdom he has shared with me over the years, and I feel so privileged to know him and have him as a friend and confidant. He has paved the way for the rest of the Berrys to follow; he truly is an icon. —**Diana Larson**

Mike Berry is a good man, a super man. He's one of the most honorable people. I would put him in an Abraham Lincoln class; he's that type of man. When Mike takes on a responsibility, he sees it through to completion. He's always out there helping people. Sometimes I get upset because some of those people don't appreciate it in the least. Sometimes they act like he owes them. They have that attitude. Some people are resentful of the power and prestige that Mike has, but he earned it. Nobody gave it to him. I tell everybody: If you want respect, you've got to earn it. —**Gerald Nassar**

I was born in Lebanon and came to the U.S. when I was five years old. As my family arrived at Detroit Metro Airport, my parents led my three brothers and me to a plaque dedicated to Michael Berry in the international terminal. My father lifted a hand towards the monument and said, 'You're in America now and you have opportunities to accomplish great things. Michael Berry's family comes from Tibnin, also, and look at how this [terminal] is named after him. He worked hard, and this is what happens when you work hard in this country.'

Every time we returned to the terminal to bid relatives good-bye or welcome relatives to the U. S., it never failed—my parents always proudly pointed out that we were standing in the Michael Berry International Terminal.

Twenty-five years later, as an English instructor at HFCC, I felt certain awe sitting in the Michael Berry Amphitheater, recalling that its benefactor [is] someone who came from the same cultural origins as my own family, a man who through his own hard work and belief in social justice had made the American dream come true—not only for himself and his family, but for so many others. **—Lara Hamza**

When you first meet Mike Berry, you don't know if you're going to like him or not, because he's tough. It's not often that Mike shoots from the hip. He usually has good reason for doing what he's doing, having thought about it. **—Mike Zolik**

People in Mike's presence were always on guard, either because they wanted to be a good example or because they did not want him to have a negative opinion of their behavior. He kept people on their toes. I don't think even Mike realized that he did that by his behavior, his demeanor, because it was out of love and respect they had for him. It wasn't like he was cracking a whip. It was the way he carried out his life and the way he lived. **—Avery Jackson, PhD**

A lot of times when you think of a powerful person, you think of someone who is kind of stoic and hard, but Mike Berry is very, very emotional. He has a great sense of humor and a great, great heart. A lot of the humanitarian things he did were anonymous. That's true giving. That's an important distinction to make. He was never one to say, I did this or I helped so and so. That is one of the qualities I admire most in him.

Mike has always been the voice of reason. He reminds me of the West African proverb made famous by President Theodore Roosevelt, Speak softly but carry a big stick; you will go far. Mike was never one for a lot of pomp and circumstance; he was pretty quiet but very wise and very effective. He knew what to do when things needed to be done. He has a clear mind. When everyone else was in chaos, he always seemed to rise above it.

One time, a controversial situation arose at the school [Geer Park

Elementary, where I am principal]. I wondered who I should contact that would make a difference and do the right thing, not just because it's politically correct. Who would rise above everything else and look at the children and what's best for them? Of course, it was Mike Berry. I called him, and we met. By golly, he just knew. He knew who to talk to, he knew the timing of when to do it, and by the end, it all unraveled and it was the best outcome for the kids. It was wonderful. He was the key person. Had he not been the one that I called, there would have been a totally different outcome. —**Andrea Awada**

If I could choose a word that symbolizes Mike Berry most it would be civility. I've seen him inculcate in the minds of those who grew up with him, myself included, a great sense of civility and how we should be supportive of our government. How you need to be decent and have a high degree of integrity, and how to get involved. He rolled up his sleeves and got involved in ways that ordinarily a person of his stature would not. Others would not find time, but he always found time.

Many have sought his wise counsel and tapped his political savvy. He was very generous, too. He donated to all of the mosques in the area, not just one. He is very cooperative with the churches. He listens well, asks the right questions, and empathizes. He proposes for people what he thinks they should do but never tells them what to do. He merely recommends that they consider doing a certain thing, that he's had experience and learned, so why would they want to reinvent the wheel? It is free now for them. Just go ahead and they will be successful.

Mike has helped a lot of people get into business by just talking to them. He encouraged them, and they would open a gas station or restaurant and become business oriented and successful as a result of his advice. He's taken people under his wing. In Islam, we have the concept of sabr (pro-active patience, like that of Job), and patience goes hand in hand with gratitude. They really become the two parts of faith. Even though Mike has been very helpful to a number of people, he doesn't wait for gratitude. He doesn't wait to get a thank you. A lot of people don't come back and thank him, but that's because they don't have the patience or the gratitude. —**Tallal (Lee) Turfe**

Michael Berry is known by many as the 'Godfather' of the Arab American community. It is said with reverence for his broad and significant influence with Arab Americans and also out of respect for his many layers of leadership in the metro area. When I came to the Roundtable, he and Jack Smith (CEO of General Motors) were chosen as the honorees for our Humanitarian Tribute in December 1996. That successful event jump-started my tenure at the Michigan Roundtable for Diversity and Inclusion. Many times since, I have gone to Michael Berry for advice and counsel; he always has responded generously and with strategic insight.

I look forward to reading his book that will unlock some of his secrets as a leader and his skill at developing important collaboratives. Hopefully, we will also get a glimpse at how he has managed to stay the course over many decades in his quest for social justice for all people.
—Rev. Daniel Krichbaum, Ph.D.

In 1996, I attended a dinner when Michael and Jack F. Smith, Jr., Chairman and CEO of General Motors were given humanitarian awards. Mr. Smith and Mr. Berry. To be in that class, in my book, is an honor. Not everybody gets to rub elbows with a General Motors chairman. Mike did. **—Frank Bewick, publisher, *Dearborn Times Herald***

Chapter 23

Michael Berry has received enough awards, commendations, and medals to fill another book. Some of those rewards for service and humanitarianism are worthy of special note.

"There are times, I'm sure," says Russ Gibb, "when Mike shakes his head at what's going on in the Middle East. He feels for his relatives over there, but he also understands how good this country has been to a boy from the wrong side of the tracks called Michael Berry."

The following honors reflect consensus of admiration and respect for Michael Berry and his countless charitable and humanitarian contributions to his community, state, nation, and the world.

International Institute Foundation
November 8, 2006
International Institute Hall of Fame Award
[Founded in 1984, the International Hall of Fame was created by the International Institute Foundation to honor recognized leaders from various ethnic backgrounds who have made outstanding contributions to the American way of life, who have demonstrated their concerned commitment to multiculturalism, and who have generously supported ethnic and cultural traditions. Honorees come from many walks of life, including medicine, education, law, science, journalism, and entrepreneurships, as well as government, industry, labor, and religion. Portraits of annual inductees are on permanent display in the second floor atrium of Detroit's Cobo Center.]

Henry Ford Community College
Michael Berry Amphitheater
Dearborn, Michigan
October 28, 2003
Dedication
[At the dedication of the Michael Berry Amphitheater, United States Congressman John Dingell further honored Michael Berry with a tribute from the United States House of Representatives.]

Real Life Children's Ranch
Northern Florida
October 2003
Major donor

Davenport University
Foundation Board of Trustees
August 22, 2003
Honoring Mike Berry, Trustee Emeritus

Michael Berry Career Center
Dearborn Heights
April 26, 2005

The Fr. Clement H. Kern Foundation
1999
In recognition of a life filled with humanitarian works and service to the people of Michigan

Lebanese American Heritage Club
October 29, 1999
For his dedication, devotion, and service to our community and for his relentless efforts in advocating our case for fairness, justice, and equality

Michigan Supreme Court
October 18, 1999
Congratulations for 50 years of service
[Mike's retirement from law practice]

Detroit College of Law
At Michigan State University
National Alumni Association
May 31, 1998
1998 Distinguished Alumni Award
[Graduate, Class 1950]

Ellis Island Medal of Honor
May 9, 1998
[The Ellis Island Medal of Honor was established in 1986 to pay tribute to the ancestral groups that comprise America's unique cultural mosaic. It is awarded to U. S. citizens from various ethnic backgrounds. Honorees are awarded for showing outstanding qualities in their personal and professional lives, yet maintaining the richness of their particular heritage. Held each May on Ellis Island, the ceremony is full of pageantry, grandeur, and emotion. The Medal of Honor is recognized by the United States House of Representatives and Senate, and as such the names of all winners are listed in the Congressional Record. Notable Medal honorees include six U. S. presidents, as well as Nobel Prize winners and leaders of industry, education, the arts, sports, and government.]

City of Dearborn
Mike Guido, Mayor
May 5, 1998
Congratulations on receiving the Ellis Island Award

Detroit College of Business
Dearborn, Michigan
May 31, 1997
Community Service Award
For distinguished service to the community and in recognition of the high esteem in which he is held by his peers and by the institution

City of Dearborn
Mike Guido, Mayor
February 5, 1997
Congratulations upon receiving the National Human Relations Award

National Conference on Community & Justice
December 1996
National Human Relations Award
Shared with John F. Smith, Jr., Former Chairman, CEO & President, General Motors Corporation

State of Michigan
John M. Engler, Governor
July 4, 1996
In grateful recognition for outstanding contributions to community, arts, history, charity...on the 110th anniversary of the United States of America

The Inter-County Highway Commission
Of Southeastern Michigan
October 27, 1995
Certificate of recognition of service
1974-1975

Islamic Center of America
Human Resources Committee
October 7, 1995
For outstanding achievements and services
to the Islamic community

American Arab & Chaldean Council
December 1994
Entrepreneur of the Year Award

National Order of Cedar of Lebanon
By the Lebanese Government
[The National Order of Cedar of Lebanon,
created by law on December 31, 1936, is
awarded in five grades for "great services
rendered to Lebanon, for acts of courage and
devotion of great moral value, as for years in
public service." The first award of the Order
to Lebanese nationals may only be made in
the grade of knight, while non-Lebanese
may be appointed to any of the grades.]

Sir Michael Berry Designation
*"Lebanon, the Republic of Lebanon, the National
Cedar Medal, the President of the Lebanese
Republic. Presented according to section law
number 3296, 3-15-93, the lawyer Mr. Michael
Berry, the National Cedar Medal, Rank Farris
(Knight). It is his right beginning from this date
3-15-93 to wear/adorn this medal as well as have
the right for such a medal and all the privileges
offered by this medal. Signed and registered under
the number 3296, Secretary Council of Medals,
Signature: Nabih Abu Faysal, Name: Nabih
Abu Faysal, on 3-16-93. Dean of the Council of
Medals, Signature: Mahmoud Oathman, name:
Mahmoud Oathman. The Lebanese Republic."*

*Michael Berry
& Congressman
John Dingell,
1993 event
honoring this
award*

*MichaelBerry&
Circuit Court
Judge George
T. Martin,
1993*

*L to R:
Tallal Turfe,
Neemat
Turfe, Bette
Misuraca,
1993*

American Lebanese Syrian Associated Charities [ALSAC]
1980
Lawyer of the Year
[The American Lebanese Syrian Associated Charities is the fund-raising arm of St. Jude Children's Research Hospital, founded by actor and humanitarian, Danny Thomas.]

Ronald Reagan, President
1980
Citation signed by Ronald Reagan, President
George H. W. Bush, Vice-President
For outstanding work handling the transportation for delegates from around the country coming to Detroit for the 1980 GOP National Convention

Jimmy Carter, President
January 13-17, 1980
White House Conference on Small Business
In appreciation for his outstanding contributions

George H. W. Bush, President
1979
Gift of presidential cufflinks with the Great Seal of the United States

City of Dearborn
Jack O'Reilly, Mayor
November 16, 1979
Michael Berry Day
Contributions and achievements noted, including 30 years of service to the Democratic Party: We are proud of Mike Berry as a self-made man who stands as a shining role model for children and adults.

*Actor
Danny
Thomas
& Michael
Berry,
1958,
Fundraiser
for Lebanese
refugees*

Danny Thomas Award
1979
In recognition of outstanding efforts in furthering the goals of St. Jude Children's Research Hospital as a member of the Board of Directors and Board of Governors
1974-1979

Wayne County Road Commission
November 16, 1979
Testimonial Resolution

Teamsters Union
Robert Holmes, Sr., President
November 16, 1979
Testimonial Resolution
For services to the people of Wayne County

Michael Berry International Terminal
Detroit Metropolitan Airport
1974
Dedication

Jack Carlisle, PR
The Dean of All Reporters
Letter to Frank Angelo, Editor,
Detroit Free Press
July 30, 1974

Dear Frank Angelo…
As one old pro to another old pro in the newspaper trade, that was a delightful column you hammered out in your inimitable style of objectivity about Mike Berry. You had him down pat. For some time, I thought there was a good story in Mike, and I am glad you tracked it down. Mike is indeed a rare public servant. He has class and he has brains and he also has intellectual incorruptibility. Of course, on paper there is no way that galloping bureaucracy known as the Wayne County Road Commission could exist with efficiency – and then Mike Berry was invented. Nobody but you has ever publicly given him and his Road Commission achievements deserving applause. I congratulate you on doing something well worthwhile for a well worthwhile public servant. …Sincerely, Jack Carlisle

Dearborn Bank & Trust
Board of Trustees
1972-1979
Member

United Auto Workers
Bard Young, Director
Staff of UAW Region 1E
1971
For his long and faithful service and friendship to the UAW and the trade union movement

Cedars Club of Lansing
August 3, 1968
Distinguished Service Citation

U. S. Information Agency
April 1966
Exemplary First Generation Lebanese
American

Appointment to Public Administrator
Tom Cavanagh, Attorney General
Signed by Irvin B. Feldman
January 1961

Michigan State Board of Governors
January 8, 1960
On Michael Berry's election to elector of
President and Vice President of United
States
Presidential Elections 1960

Dearborn Township
Attorney
January 13, 1953 – March 12, 1957

Private Pilot's License
July 1940

New Beginnings

Yesterday is but today's memory;
and tomorrow is today's dream.

—Kahlil Gibran

Chapter 24

No book does justice to a living, breathing human being. One must have the privilege of sitting with that person, sharing, laughing, crying, discussing – splitting a dish of ice cream – to really know who that person is. That is especially true of a gentle giant like Michael Berry. Not only because he is still very much alive, but also because he remains active in legal, political, educational, and humanitarian circles, this biography becomes a living, ongoing chronicle of Michael Berry's life. New chapters will be added one day to complete it, but in the meantime, consider it as incomplete as one's life, as long as one continues to live and breathe.

The stories contained in this book are infinitesimally small, compared to those that comprise Michael Berry's life. It would indeed take volumes to tell the whole story and to continue telling stories that unfold almost daily as we write. To a person, everyone interviewed for this book has offered hopes that Michael Berry will live for many more years; there in an inexplicable attachment they have for his presence in their lives.

And so Michael Berry has plans.

As the old Karen Carpenter song says, "We've only just begun to live…" this biography is, in a real sense, just beginning. We have barely tapped the surface of Michael Berry's lifetime achievements in his 86 years on planet Earth, and we have a great deal to look forward to as the years unfold.

Michael Berry has plans!

As many of the contributors to this book who know Michael will tell you, he has incredible stamina, a very young heart, a good sense of humor, and health that would be the envy of many people much younger than he is. Some suggest genetics set the stage for his longevity; others claim that his adherence to the Mediterranean diet, touted by such notable publications as Prevention magazine as the world's healthiest cuisine, is responsible for Michael's youthful appearance and strong constitution.

Like the Energizer bunny, he fully intends to keep ticking for as long as possible. You will be hearing more from him and more about him in the future.

Michael Berry has plans.

In addition to continuing to serve on numerous boards, he maintains strong ties to his legal profession, occasionally serving in a consultant capacity on a case or offering legal assistance on a pro bono basis.

In addition to keeping up socially with friends and associates, Michael married Cindy Hanes on April 14, 2007, enjoyed a delayed honeymoon, and visited his daughter, Cindi, and her husband, Raymond, in Arizona. From there, your guess is as good as mine. Surely, some new project will beckon him, and again he will not be able to resist helping someone in need or some worthy cause that could benefit from his wisdom, expertise or support.

In addition to all of these commitments, his activities with family always take center-stage, especially where his sons are concerned. Keeping up with the boys (Timothy and Brendan) helps keep Michael young, too.

Just as we can learn from Michael's living legacy, we should embrace life with the same gusto that he demonstrates, always looking for opportunities to serve and to share, ways to give and to care.

Wake up every day with a dream; retire each night, being thankful for that day and looking forward to tomorrow. Maintain a positive attitude and determination to make this world a better place for future generations. Pay tribute to the one who has made an indelible mark on countless lives, who has challenged people of all ages to strive for the best, and who has shown the way to a fulfilling and rewarding life by following his example.

As these last words are written, Michael Berry starts a new chapter of his life.

Michael Berry has plans.

Selfishly or unselfishly, we hope and pray that he lives long enough to fulfill these plans and many more.

Insha Allah.

About the Author

Writing has always come easily for Susan Giffin. In her senior English class at Farmington High School, she wrote a 15,000-word biography about a Hungarian refugee. [*Michael Berry* exceeds 64,000 words.] Susan received her BA in English from Berea College in Berea, Kentucky. There, she served as the news editor of the college paper.

Susan worked with the world's greatest literacy expert, the late Dr. Frank Laubach, in Syracuse, New York. At that time, she had an eye-opening experience, teaching a 35-year-old illiterate to read and write his native language—English. A few years later, Susan wrote about that experience for *Good Housekeeping* magazine long before literacy came into vogue. The publisher, John Mack Carter, loved the article, but eventually decided not to publish it because no one could find Susan's student to obtain permission to run his photograph.

For the next 20 years, Susan concentrated on medical public relations and writing; first with the American College of Surgeons in Chicago and a few years later in Dearborn, for Dr. Stanley Grandon, one of the world's leading eye surgeons. She traveled to the USSR to interview the ophthalmologist who developed radial keratotomy, and later wrote Good-bye, Glasses, the first consumer guide to that breakthrough surgery.

A few years ago, Susan decided to step outside the medical writing box and enrolled in a screenwriting course with Harvey Ovshinsky, then Detroit's dean of screenwriting; during that six-month course, she wrote a feature film screenplay, which is currently under development in California. From there, Susan continued to open new doors to her life-long dream: writing books. To date, Susan has ghostwritten, authored, and edited more than 35 books for clients all over the world.

Susan resides in Dearborn with her cat, Sylvester.

Printed in the United States
95906LV00004B/181-279/A